Redeemed by Love

Redeemed by Love

Reflections on Survival

BettyJo Cost

iUniverse, Inc.
New York Bloomington

Redeemed by Love

Reflections on Survival

Copyright © 2008 by BettyJo Cost

iUniverse books may be ordered through booksellers or by contacting:

iUniverse
1663 Liberty Drive
Bloomington, IN 47403
www.iuniverse.com
1-800-Authors (1-800-288-4677)

ISBN: 978-0-595-52585-0 (pbk)
ISBN: 978-0-595-62639-7 (ebk)

Printed in the United States of America

iUniverse rev. date: 12/04/09

Contents

Acknowledgments

The following memoir is dedicated to my precious sister, Mary Elizabeth, and to my loving brother, Charles Stanley. These pages are your voice as well as mine.

And to my beloved daughters Shelley and Nancy, who have always brought great warmth to my heart, even when I wasn't as loving a mother as I should have been.

I am grateful to David Brooks Andrews, whose talent made the cover of this book possible, and whose professional assistance in editing made these pages more readable.

And I owe so much to two precious friends from my youth—Beverly Hustead Shell and the Honorable Dewey Falcone—who have been tireless in their encouragement and support.

And, finally, to those who through either mental or physical abuse have had their innocence, dignity, and sense of self-worth brutally taken from them, may you have the insight and courage necessary to reclaim the qualities that are rightfully yours; may your famished emotions feel the peace you deserve; and may you finally be healed!

Introduction

For as long as I can remember, man's inhumanity to man has deeply saddened me. His often indulgent, self-seeking interests—with no regard to cruel, remorseless acts and how they affect the lives of so many—are fully evidenced in the news media every hour of every day.

Questions as to why adversities exist and an insatiable need to understand life's purpose began in my early childhood.

These issues motivated me to seek something more—to understand how it might be possible to become the good person I longed to see in others.

This yearning led me to question if it's actually possible for people to change and improve their character, as a means of controlling their self-indulgent behavior.

The following disclosure is the result of this lifelong inquiry.

Secrecy and servitude consumed the first eighteen years of my life. Though appearances of family and home were present, I was bound in complete subjection and physical restraint to the will of another human being, making home the reverse of what it appeared to be.

Pretending it was normal and healthy, I lived in constant fear that someone would see my shame and accuse me of contributing to it.

I was terrified of my stepfather! Though I didn't want to hate my mother, her denial, alcoholism and inability to protect her three children contributed to those feelings.

The head of our household, the protagonist in the first part of my story, was a pedophile. The sordid details, however, are not what this book is about. And I want to be very clear here: My motive in revealing this is to share healing, not to seek commiseration. Sharing my experience isn't something I've wanted to do, but rather what I've felt led to do.

Should these pages bring a sense of renewal and regeneration to your life, dear reader, they have accomplished what was intended. If they serve to replace an inner void with hope and bring your grief nearer closure, then sharing these facts is worthwhile.

Perhaps one of the most miraculous results of my life's experience is that forgiveness and balance came about not through therapy or psychiatry, but through a conscious effort to examine my thinking in an attempt to discern how one's thought affects experience.

To achieve this, I educated myself spiritually, giving specific attention to explanations concerning the so-called dark side of human nature. The goodness and beauty in human character made sense as opposed to the malignity of brutal predators. Injustice could not quench the famished need to know God as Love. A presence and intelligence greater than self motivated my search.

During my experience, and in spite of willingness to look beyond self, suicide sometimes seemed tempting, as the only possible way of silencing pain. Regardless of the presence of grief and fear, my search continued, and I was led through prayer on a humble path of asking God questions and listening intently for answers. Listening became constant due to several mysterious physical healings experienced when I was three, eight, and twelve years old. Those healings left me with the desire to understand how it's possible to heal illness without relying on material remedies.

The following vignettes will illustrate obstacles to stability, show how those obstacles were overcome, and how healing resulted. They will touch on the adversities, but only as they illustrate healing. Freedom came thought by thought over my lifetime, as a result of learning to imbibe deeper views of God and man through reason and understanding. Reading through these events perhaps you will agree with Shakespeare as I do: "Sweet are the uses of adversity."

Los Angeles Children's Hospital

Physical Healing

While swinging in the backyard one day, I suddenly became unconscious. When I woke up, I was lying across my mother's lap in a car being driven by a neighbor. The destination was the Los Angeles Children's Hospital.

I blacked out a second time. When I regained consciousness, I was in a children's ward. It was 1934, and I was three years old.

I could turn my head in both directions, but there was no movement in the rest of my body. I was paralyzed from the shoulders down. When I looked to the right and to the left, I could see long rows of white cribs. I couldn't see any motion except for the movement of an arm of the child in the crib next to mine.

His arm was extended outward and upward and moved back and forth as though he was going to throw something.

There was a small, white object in his hand. It looked like a paper airplane. I remember thinking, "If he throws it and it lands on the floor, he won't be able to get up to get it." And then my thought said back to me, "But that is not going to happen to me!"

The diagnosis was infantile paralysis. There was an epidemic of polio running rampant in the '30s. No treatments were available in those days, outside of warm baths and the process of attempting to walk while holding on to railings.

I left the hospital wearing braces on my legs. A short time later when the braces were removed, the attending physician said to my mother, "This is a miracle! This child has been healed of polio."

The importance of these events is the thought that refused to accept the condition. Refusing to accept polio as permanent and belonging to me was the key. In its own time, my body adjusted to my protestations. Later in my experience, I realized it was God who healed me, but, of course, I had no idea as to how.

I've had friends say no one can remember thoughts that occurred to them at that age. My answer to their remark has always been: When God's healing presence speaks to human consciousness, one cannot forget!

One of the ways God speaks to us is through our prayers. I believe the prayers of those praying for victims of the polio epidemic during the '30s reached all receptive thought. Their prayers certainly reached mine.

This healing of polio was the first of three so-called miraculous healings that took place during my early childhood.

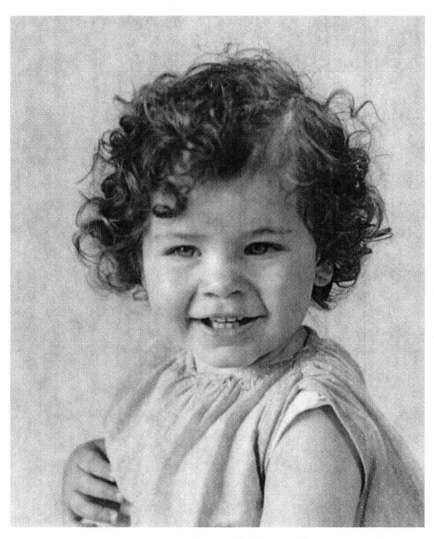

BettyJo as a young child in 1934

Living in a Store

Predator in the House

We moved from Los Angeles in 1935 into a building in Redondo Beach that had been used as a grocery store during the '20s and early '30s. The building was square with the usual storefront facade of the early 1900s. Inside was a large, single room with a small, dark kitchen and bath. Heavy white draperies hung from ceiling rods, creating floating walls for a visual separation of rooms.

At four years of age, I was still sleeping in a crib. One night I woke to hands moving all over my body. The feeling was one of horror! I screamed, and the hands pulled away. I called my mother, but she didn't come, so I crawled out of bed and went to her curtained room.

Quick movement out of the crib was possible due to the lowered railing. Tucking me in for the night, mother had raised it, but it had since been lowered.

As I stood at her bedside sobbing, mother asked why I was crying. I told her, "Daddy put his hands all over me!" She told me I had been dreaming and sent me back to bed. That so-called dream is as vivid today as it was the night it happened.

Kindergarten

Appetite

Rushing to work one morning, my dad forgot to take his lunch, so mother sent the brown bag with me to school. It had a banana and a candy bar in it. Tasting a banana and a candy bar for the first time remains unforgettable.

It was 1936, and food was still a scarcity. That lunch bag for me has always brought sweet memories, though perhaps it was that very moment when I began sacrificing nutrition for pleasurable tastes.

Sometime when I was between the ages of five and six, we moved from the former store. On the day of the move, mother asked me to get breakfast for my brother and sister, who were younger than I.

Mother explained that white cereal was on the stove in a large pot. She told me to dish it up and put sugar and milk on it for each of us. I did as she asked. I put the cereal into bowls, got the milk out of the icebox, and called my brother and sister to the table.

Returning to the kitchen, mother asked, "Why aren't you eating your breakfast?" We all started crying. "We can't eat it," I said. "Why is that?" she asked. "It tastes funny," I answered. Mother became angry and finally tasted the cereal. She turned to me and yelled, "Where did you get this?"

I showed her the pot on the stove. It was just as she described, a large pot filled with white cereal. "That's not cereal," mother shouted. "It's lard!"

Mother failed to remember that she had two pots on the stove, each filled with something white.

Mary McNellis

A Good Person

When Mary McNellis Fondren brushed her hair at night, it was so long it covered her hips. During the day it was neatly arranged in a bun on top of her head. She was a large woman and always wore housedresses.

Mary was my grandmother. By her early twenties, she was totally blind. Mary's adversity, however, never prevented her from completing her household chores or caring for her four children.

I was two the first time mother took me to Merced to visit Grandpa and Grandma Fondren. We took the train from Los Angeles. When we reached our destination and stepped off the train, a cow strolled slowly down the tracks toward us. I'd never seen a cow before. It was huge. I stood frozen by the train crying and screaming for mother. I've had a deep affection for cows ever since.

Mary was wife and mother like no other. Without an ability to see, she cooked meals on a woodburning stove. As a small child, I remember looking at her and wondering how she kept from burning her hands and her clothing when she reached over the front of the stove to the back burners.

Though Mary was blind, she seemed perfectly capable, without handicaps, or objectionable habits, except for one thing. Mary chewed snuff. Even for a small child, that was gross!

After her children were raised and grandfather Fondren passed on, Mary came to live with us for a short time. She had a keen sense of humor and laughed easily, so we often loved to play games with her.

One day as she was feeling her way down the hall to the necessary room, I quietly watched her. After knocking and receiving no response, Mary opened the bathroom door, felt the countertop and commode to make sure no one was there.

Before she closed the door, I scooted around her body and curled up in a corner waiting for just the right moment.

Mary pulled up her dress and pulled down her bloomers exposing her huge pink bottom. During that split second, I pulled my tiny body up and sat on the commode. She came down on me like a battleship destined for home. When the two of us met, she screamed as though she had just been shot.

Hearing Mary's scream, mother came running down the hall shouting, "Mother, are you all right?" She knew the moment she saw me that I had been up to something.

What did Mary McNellis do to me? She laughed so hard she could barely speak. She did manage to say to my mother, however, "Ethel, don't you whop that girl!"

That was my grandmother. She was the best playmate I had my entire life. Later I wondered why that was, and the answer came as a revelation.

Mary was incapable of anger and hate. My grandmother was pure love, all love. What an incredible example. Memory of my grandmother has always brought joy to my heart.

From left to right: George Edward Fondren, his wife, Mary McNellis
Fondren, and his brother (name unknown)

From left to right: George Edward Fondren, Mary McNellis, and their
daughters, baby Ethel, Agnes, and Nellie

E. T.

Bad Example of Motherhood

Probably due to the natural bond between mother and child, I choose to believe that most of what my mother, Ethel Fondren, was involved in was not her fault. Having no knowledge of her own worth, she was by unconscious consent a co-dependent. She was a battered woman—a victim of her husband and the times.

Though her name was Ethel, friends called mother "E.T." In 1930, she was only fifteen when she ran away from home to marry.

Mother married Doyle James Byrd on March 5, 1930. Their marriage license lists Doyle's father as John Byrd of West Virginia and his mother as Mary Edds of Ohio. Doyle was born in Tennessee.

Doyle was employed by my grandfather's nursery. Mother told me that during the Depression her father was prosperous, employing six people full-time.

Grandfather's name was George Edward Fondren. He was of French decent and born in Waco, Texas, on March 18, 1872. In the twelfth census of the United States, June 1900, George, age twenty-eight, was recorded as living in the township of Hartshorne, in the county of Choctaw Nation, in the state of Indian Territory. The report lists both of his parents as having been born in South Carolina, which makes George Edward Fondren a distant cousin to Walter William Fondren, the founder of Humble Oil, which later became Exxon.

George eventually left Texas and moved to the state of Washington. A 1910 U.S. census lists George Edward Fondren as living with his wife, Mary, in King, Washington. They moved to Merced, California after their children were born.

George's wife, Mary McNellis, was Irish. Due to cataracts, she was blind by age twenty. Her condition was inoperable. E.T. shared the fact that Mary never saw the faces of her four surviving children. Mary had six in all.

When Ethel and Doyle eloped, they moved to Madera, which left Doyle unemployed.

I was expected during the summer of 1931. Many years later, mother briefly shared something of what her life was like while she was pregnant with me during the Depression.

As a sixteen-year-old expectant mother, Ethel Fondren Byrd occasionally could be seen standing outside the local Madera Bakery salivating over aromas from fresh-baked bread and pastries coming from within.

Unable to afford more than two meals a day, E.T. was hopelessly traumatized by what she saw in the bakery window. Even the smallest loaf of bread was beyond her fiscal ability.

Mother's story left me wondering what prevented those working inside the bakery from offering her something to eat. I've visualized this unfortunate scene many times and felt such sadness for her hunger, frustration, and myself as her expected child.

I was six or seven when we moved to Curtis Avenue in Redondo Beach. Doyle Byrd came for a brief visit. He was introduced to me as my uncle.

Doyle had his wife, Martha, and their two young children with them. When the four adults went out in the evening, I was given the responsibility of caring for my brother, sister, and Doyle and Martha's two children while the adults partied.

That was the first and last time I ever saw Doyle Byrd, and I haven't seen his two children, Norma and James, my half-brother and half-sister since.

The interior of our two-story home wasn't finished at the time my mother and stepdad, Charles Earl Root, bought it in the '30s. Though the outside was completed, nothing was finished inside. The kitchen walls were plastered, but two-by-fours were exposed throughout the rest of the house. Like most homes in the '30s and '40s, it had no running hot water. The water had to be heated on the stove.

I was eight years old when, early one Easter morning, mother tripped and fell down the wooden stairs, from the second story to the bottom of the staircase. She was rushed to the hospital and returned home days later wearing a cast from her waist to her shoulders. The fall broke her back in more than one place.

In spite of the fact that the room was without draperies, E.T.'s bed was moved from the upstairs master bedroom to the downstairs living room.

While mother was still confined to bed, a young woman came to help with the household chores.

One day after the help left, mother asked me to bathe my sister. She wanted me to remove the boiling water from the stove, carry it to the kitchen sink, and combine it with cooler water to bathe Mary Elizabeth.

I did as she asked. But when I carried the heavy pail of boiling hot water to the sink and put it down on a surface a little too high to comfortably reach, it spilled all over my body and severely burned me from the waist down.

Though any movement was dangerous for mother, upon hearing my screams, she jumped out of bed and ran to the kitchen. When she saw the pail on the floor and realized what had happened, she began removing my clothes. The skin came off in large layers with the removal of my underwear.

Dad came in and insisted on taking over. Mother shouted at him in a voice full of contempt. That was the only time in my entire life I ever heard E.T. speak to her husband with authority. As I thought back on the scene later, I realized she knew more about the secrecy of his aggressions than she could safely admit.

After removing my clothes, E.T. put me in her bed and carefully spread butter all over the burned area. The pain got worse. When the doctor arrived, he told her that butter further cooked the skin, and he gently removed all of it. Afterward, he wrapped my legs and abdomen in gauze and told mother I had third degree burns over 60 percent of my body.

During that summer, I spent a lot of days and nights in pain. The doctor visited our home, and later we made several trips to his office. During one of those visits, he told my mother I wasn't healing and needed a skin graft. I asked him what that meant.

His description of the procedure was very graphic. He told me he would surgically remove skin from mother's hip, and sew it to my legs. The way he described it sounded as though her skin would literally be torn from her hips. The whole procedure suggested such cruelty that I turned to him and said, "You are not going to do that to MY mother!"

Deeply irritated, I left his office. Not long after that office visit, my legs and stomach began to heal. Later I heard the second physician say, "It's a miracle. She's healing."

Many times over the years, I've thought back on this experience. I believe the key to the healing was twofold. First, a stand was taken against the surgical procedure. It just didn't sound right. Secondly, I refused to let mother go through the process because I felt such love for her and was convinced the procedure would hurt her. From that point on, my body began to heal. The stand for a higher solution changed the physical condition.

My legs and stomach healed without scarring, except for one large scar high up on my thigh. Fortunately, as I grew older, the scar wasn't noticeable in the bathing suit style of the '40s.

During WWII, my stepdad was in the Merchant Marines. While he was gone it was the most peaceful, beautiful time my brother, sister, and I ever experienced with our mother.

I can still visualize E.T. standing by a window near the front door on Curtis Avenue fixing her hair and makeup. She was somewhat attractive. What made her unattractive was a severe overbite. Her dental condition was called buckteeth. This type of bite was common in the '40s, and preceded orthodontia. Exquisite as she was in her films, Jean Tierney also had the same type of occlusion.

Late one afternoon, mother was getting ready to go to work. She was employed by Douglas Aircraft as a draftsperson and worked on blueprints for airplanes. I remember looking at her with affection as she stood by the window watching for her afternoon ride to the plant in El Segundo.

I have no idea why she switched from blueprints to repairing bicycles, but by the time I was twelve she was working at a bicycle shop on Pier Avenue in Hermosa Beach.

One day, around four in the afternoon, when E.T. was due home from work, I noticed our 1931 Model A was still in the driveway. Apparently she couldn't get it started and managed to get to work some other way.

Suddenly, I felt responsible. I knew I had to find a way to get the car cranked and started so I could pick her up from work. The fact that I didn't know how to drive wasn't even a concern. I felt it was my responsibility.

I asked my brother and sister to help push the car out of the dirt driveway and onto the street. A neighbor saw us and asked if he could help. "Yes," I said. "Can you drive?" he asked. "Of course," I replied. He then told us to get in the car while he pushed. We did, and as he pushed us the car started.

I turned left on Prospect and drove toward Aviation Boulevard. Turning right on Aviation, we were headed toward Hermosa Beach. By imitating the foot action of my parents when they drove, I somehow managed to get the car in gear. By this time Mary and Chuck were so frightened they were down on the floor.

They were up on the seat again by the time we arrived at Pier Avenue. Mother was standing on the corner waiting and watching for someone. She noticed the car, and then she saw the three of us. As I turned left on Pier Avenue, E.T., in a state of panic, started screaming and running down the hill. Her mouth was wide open. Her arms were swinging wildly in the air.

The hill was steep, and suddenly it occurred to me that, although I had managed to get the car in gear, I didn't know how to stop it. The hill seemed to get steeper. Then I became frightened. Mary and Chuck were sobbing. They knew I didn't know how to stop the car.

It suddenly occurred to me to turn right into the curb, and the curb would force the car to stop. That is what happened. The car bounced up over the curb, coughed, and came to a complete stop.

We were successful that day in bringing our mother home. I wasn't scolded for my efforts, but driving lessons were on the household agenda almost immediately. At the age of twelve, I had absolutely no idea of the danger I had caused the three of us. I just knew getting mother home was my responsibility.

I've often wondered how much of E.T.'s addiction to alcohol was due to the frustration and despair over her marriage to her second husband, due to so-called genetics, or due to both. Ethel Fondren was cruelly battered and her face badly disfigured by Charles Root during their marriage.

A comment made by a nephew after Chuck's funeral led me to believe that mother may have been involved in abusing my brother. If she was a pedophile, it may have been because she was forced to do what her husband told her or risk another brutal beating. Though I don't have firsthand information, as I have in my own case and my sister's, I was witness to the fact that every time something strange involving my brother was going on in our home, mother was with those who seemed to disappear.

In addition to caring for her home, Ethel worked all during our childhood. I don't believe there was ever a time when she didn't have a job. Sometimes her drinking binges prevented her from working, but since they usually occurred on the weekends, she rarely missed more than an occasional Monday.

I hated the alcohol consumed and the ugly cigarettes always hanging from the corner of her mouth. There wasn't any education while I was growing up about secondhand smoke and how it affects people's lives.

After E.T. had only one or two glasses of wine, somehow I could always tell she was on her way to becoming drunk. Once she started, she seemed to have absolutely no control. The alcohol often made her violently ill. Afterward she would promise my brother, my sister, and me that she would never do it again. The promises always became lies.

When my mother and stepdad partied or when mother was ill, it was up to me to be the caretaker. I learned at a very early age to pick up the clothing thrown on the floor, make the beds, clean up in general, and watch and feed my brother and sister. Children of addicts are often placed in a caretaker position.

One of the things I detested the most about their lifestyle was the abundance of alcohol and tobacco, while the food we needed for proper nourishment was occasionally lacking.

While her husband was with her, I purposely had little or no communication with E.T. Once he passed on, I still rarely contacted her. After both my brother and sister passed on, it was up to me to care for her when she became ill.

In her late sixties, E.T. came to stay with us in Pebble Beach. She had lung cancer and liver complications.

It was very hard to have her in my home. Our issues were unresolved, so it was difficult even to attempt a conversation with her. I didn't have any conscious rage left in my heart, but I had a lot of questions. She was still so much in denial, however, that it was impossible to communicate naturally with her.

Though she never spoke of my brother or sister, she made references to her husband, Charles, several times. I asked her not to mention his name in my home. She asked, "Why?" I said, "Because he was an awful man! He molested me, Mary, and Chuck." Her remark was, "I don't believe anything I haven't seen!" I just looked at her in profound disgust and amazement.

I thought, "She doesn't believe me." Turning to her, I said, "It doesn't matter to me that you refuse to acknowledge the fact that he was a sexual predator. I am living proof he was, and nothing can hide that fact any longer. Your denial or refusal to see and admit the truth can't change the facts. He ruined my life and the lives of my sister and brother. He ruined your life. He took something beautiful and turned it into a living hell. He was the scum of the earth! Had laws against pedophiles been in place soon enough, he would have served his remaining years in prison, because I would have put him there."

In one last effort to help her acknowledge what I knew she obviously knew, I turned to her and said, "You consciously chose to be blind to the harm your children were experiencing."

In obvious reaction to what she had just heard and in a tone of hatred, mother glanced around at our well furnished, six-thousand-square-foot home and said, "It takes a lot to make you happy, Betty!"

I replied, "No, mother. It doesn't take materiality to make me happy. Our home and the things we own are the result of how hard we've worked. What it took to make you happy, however, was the alcohol, nicotine, sensuality, and enabling role you lived as the wife of a pedophile. It took sacrificing the innocence, emotional stability, and the wellness of your children to make you happy, Ethel! Our emotional stability and safety was exchanged for a roof over your head and a man at your side. And you've remained in denial about this fact all your life. You aren't even acknowledging these facts now, and you know full well that they are true. No, mother, it took far more to make you happy."

Though tears rolled down her cheeks, she didn't say a word. I was so upset that I had to leave the room. That was the only time I revealed my feelings openly to her. After all that had been said, Ethel offered no comment. Her silence seemed to me to be an admission. She appeared to continue to choose denial rather than face what she had become. But, thank God, I was given a chance to say what I had been forced to suppress all those years.

After confronting E.T., I recalled a remark a friend, Rosalie Fritzen, made during one of our high school reunions. I apologized to Rosalie for not remaining in touch after graduation and tried briefly to explain the traumatic childhood I was still working through. She immediately reminded me of the time when we were fourteen and she was invited to spend the night at my home. Before retiring, and while we were bathing, Rosalie asked me to lock the bathroom door. "You told me we couldn't lock the door because your dad wouldn't allow it." She said, "Before we finished bathing, he came in, spoke while staring at both of us and then left." Her reason for never wanting to stay in my home again was because he terrified her.

How could E.T. not have known that her husband demanded the bathroom doors be left unlocked? How could she have missed the fact that he entered the bathroom when her children needed privacy? Though I was never able to prove it, Ethel obviously knew what Charles was about, and she was an active part of it.

The confusing, hateful feelings I had to work through were common for a child living under this type of trauma. It's not unusual to blame one's mother for adversity in the home. Children do so because instinctively they know she should be protecting them.

Before long, E.T. was anxious to get back to her home in Rogue River, Oregon. Her cancer was in remission. I put her on the plane having to remind myself every step of the way to treat her with patience and love. Weeks later the dance with cancer began all over again. This time she was taken to the hospital in Medford, Oregon.

It was the early part of the '80s, and my husband, James Peter Cost, was running for California State Assembly. He was a Republican candidate running against a Democrat incumbent. We had fundraising to do, and needed at least two hundred and fifty thousand dollars to meet expenses just for the campaign.

The calls to be by E.T.'s side were very serious, so I flew back and forth to the hospital trying to take care of mother in the most loving way I possibly could. On one hand, I was angry with her for not taking care of her health, and, on the other hand, I understood. She led a life full of fear and torment. As a human being, she had serious problems. But wasn't she a victim of the times? There was no outside help for crimes committed within the home.

There were no facilities to care for battered women and sexually abused children. All issues of sexual perversion remained in secrecy. Any discussion of sexual assault against children was unheard of. Revealing such events could have put our lives at further risk—hers and ours. For the moment, I let go of the contempt I felt for her lifestyle and began to come up with a solution for caring for her on a daily basis.

I opted to fly her from Medford, Oregon to Monterey, California, and take her to the Carmel Valley Hospice, where I had made previous arrangements for her care. Once she was there, I could visit E.T. often.

A Mercy Flight was hired. The plane was small. There was room only for the pilot, his copilot, the nurse, E.T., and me. When we were in the air, the nurse told me something strange. She whispered, "If your mother dies during the flight, do not tell the pilot. Whatever you do, don't let him know."

At this point, the pilot turned to speak to the nurse, so I continued stroking E.T.'s head. I told her I loved her, and she replied, "I love you too." To help her relax more, I rubbed her arms and lightly stroked her forehead.

I was extremely tired. The campaign kept me up every evening frequently until two or three a.m. I was helping plan parties, giving them for fundraising or writing letters on our AB Dick computer to friends, fellow Republicans, clients, and anyone I could think of to raise funds. I was also running the gallery—the James Peter Cost Gallery—full time and had the needs of my youngest daughter, Nancy, to care for. When I saw mother resting, I put my head back and fell asleep.

The nurse woke me a short time later and whispered, "Your mother has passed on." Considering what she told me earlier, I reached for mother's head and continued stroking it. I also bent over and quietly told her goodbye. I didn't have a single tear. I felt relieved. But to make sure the pilot didn't discover what had taken place, I continued to lean over to talk to E.T.

During this time, the most amazing thing took place. All residual anger, hatred, feelings of disgust, and resentment I had felt over the past fifty-one years suddenly disappeared. Something else had taken their place.

From the moment mother passed on, the only feelings present were those of love. The bond of mother and daughter was fully present. Love filled my heart and consciousness with love. God was indeed filling all space with His/Her Motherly Love, goodness, presence, and unspeakable peace.

After the plane landed at the Monterey Airport and we all got out, I told the pilot my mother had passed on. He asked when it happened. I told him exactly what the nurse told me to say. I replied, "Just as we were landing." With that information, he called the coroner, and E.T. was taken directly to Paul Mortuary in Pacific Grove.

As soon as the coroner left, I asked the nurse why she wanted me to keep mother's demise from the pilot. Her answer was surprising. "Had you told him earlier, he would have had to land the plane in the county over which she died. We could have been detained there for days, or at least until the legal papers were completed." I was relieved to know I had carefully followed her instructions, for I was needed at home.

When I returned home from the airport, JP and Nancy Pamela were waiting for me. I phoned ahead to explain the delay and to tell them the details of what had taken place. They were very concerned and supportive.

Once home, I found I had another dilemma. How was I going to get E.T. back to Rogue River to fulfill her wish to be buried in the plot next to her husband, Charles? My niece offered me her station wagon, so I decided to drive mother's body back to Oregon. I called the mortuary and gave them the following instructions: "Please prepare the body, embalm it, and dress my mother back in the clothes she was wearing, including her rubber shoes. Put her in a cardboard box. Since it will be less expensive, I'll purchase a casket in Oregon. Please call me and let me know how soon you can have her body ready."

Our personal funds were running short. The activities of the campaign kept JP away from the easel all that year and most of the next. Except for a few originals I had saved for our retirement, we had no paintings to sell at the gallery to meet our personal needs and business expenses. Driving mother's body back to her final resting place was a great deal more affordable than flying. Within two days, I was ready to leave for Oregon once again.

I was fully prepared to go alone. I asked my niece, Denise Barber, who lived in Carmel Valley, if she would join me, but she didn't want to be in the car with a cadaver. JP had no intentions of going along. However, at the last minute, rather than have me drive alone, he decided to go. His company was a great relief.

We had to arrive at the morgue in Oregon by midnight. Arriving by twelve meant that the morticians would still be on the premises, and would remove the body from the car. We could then be free to spend the night without wondering what we were going to do with E.T.

JP told ghost stories during the entire drive from Monterey to Rogue River, Oregon. When he worked at it, he was really funny. At one point he actually had me convinced that the cardboard box had opened, and E.T. was sitting up. His humor didn't let up. He entertained me during the nine hundred or so miles to the mortuary.

When we drove back to the Monterey Peninsula with my niece, who had flown from Monterey to Oregon for the funeral, he continued to tell amazingly funny stories.

Gratitude frequently comes to me when I think of E.T. I'm grateful to her for showing me qualities in the human character I would never want to exemplify or claim as my own.

More than any other person, mother gave me reasons to learn to forgive. I never forgave her ignorance, immorality, or selfishness—her behavior, but I did learn through prayer and spiritual study to separate the error from the person.

Through all that sadness, mother truly gave me the ultimate gift—the need to grow spiritually. That fact is something I've been immensely grateful for. If she had known how to be a better human being, I choose to believe she would have been. My heart still aches for the fragile, unfortunate woman she became.

When the movie *E. T.* came to theaters, I rushed to see it. I loved it, and came away with the feeling that Ethel Fondren was the original E.T. I still continue to feel only love, tenderness, and compassion for mother. She led a pitiful existence, which provided the example and motivation I needed to strive for a better way of life.

From left to right: Chuck, BettyJo, and Ethel Fondren Root

Our home on Curtis Avenue, Redondo Beach, during the 1940s

Hungry for a Father's Genuine Love

Teenage Promiscuity

I first saw Ron Harrod walking toward me in the high school science building. His hair was dark and wavy. His shirt was white and crisp. His jeans were impeccably pressed. He looked as though he had just stepped out of an Asian laundry.

Our eyes met, and it wasn't just a glance. It was as though we saw something magnificently profound within one another.

The movement of his body had a unique spirit and sprint as he passed by. He was the most handsome person I had ever seen! Fortunately, I had the composure to keep from turning around as he strode further down the hall.

It was 1945. I was fourteen and a high school freshman. Ron was sixteen and a junior. I saw him again for the second time not too long after our eyes first met. He pulled into our driveway in his new '46 black Mercury Coupe. He came to the door to ask if he could take me out.

We started seeing one another when I was too young to date seriously. As far as my parents were concerned, however, I wasn't too young. My mother was married at fifteen and had me by the time she was sixteen. She wasn't the least bit reluctant to send me into the arms of a young man eager to claim his manhood.

We lived in North Redondo on Curtis Avenue just a few doors off what was then Prospect Avenue. North Redondo was considered the other side of the tracks. Most of the students at Redondo Union High School lived in Palos Verdes Estates, Manhattan, Hermosa or Redondo Beach proper.

I was embarrassed about where we lived. That fact probably had more to do with the way I felt about my parents, however, than the location of our home.

I never revealed to Ron what was taking place at home. I was too terrified to mention the details to anyone. Discussions of that magnitude never occurred in the '40s. And the predator went to great measures to make sure we were too frightened to ever talk about the events with anyone, even with one another. Don Miguel Ruiz reveals these feelings in his book, *The Mastery of Love*, in the following way: "Domestication can be so strong and the wounds so deep that you can even be afraid to speak."

Starved for affection, I was eager to receive the attention Ron was more than willing to give. His was the first love I ever experienced. He embraced me with such tenderness—feelings I'd never known. As I loved him, the world took on a whole new perspective. A measure of good seemed possible.

We shared similar interests and had wonderful times together. Ron was sensitive and protective. He made me feel life had purpose and value. When we ended our evenings together, it was all I could do to wait for the next.

We dated constantly during my freshman year. We saw movies at the Graumens' Chinese and Pantages Theatres. We went to Earl Carols' Nightclub in Los Angeles. We danced at the Palladium to the rhythm of the Big Bands— Les Brown, Artie Shaw, Harry James, and others.

We had our greatest times together, however, at "The Shack" located near the railroad tracks in Hermosa Beach. It was a place where RUHS students could go, buy soft drinks, and dance to the popular music of the '40s. Doris Day, Johnny Mercer, Nat King Cole, Lena Horne, Kay Star, and Hoagie Carmichael were some of our favorites.

One of our best dates was the Junior/Senior Prom. I wore a red and white flowered dress on which Ron pinned a white gardenia. It was exciting to be going to the prom. It was one of our most romantic evenings.

Sadly, my parents sold our home on Curtis Avenue that summer, and we moved from Redondo Beach further south to Hemet. Moving away seemed like the end of the world to me. I was crushed not to be living in the South Bay, so I could continue to see Ron. His love and friendship was the first good experienced in my life. I never really recovered from the pain of being separated from him. They were present companions wherever I went.

My parents had a small apricot ranch in Hemet. On occasion we took a truckload of fruit to market in Los Angeles, and at that time I was able to see Ron again.

On one of our dates, we parked in El Segundo along the ocean. A police officer came up to the door and shined a flashlight on us. We were caught in an embarrassing situation. We were terribly frightened. The officer asked our ages, to which Ron promptly replied untruths. He had the presence of mind to say, "Eighteen." After shining light in our faces, he told us to move on.

Our actions didn't seem unnatural to me. For as long as I could remember, physicality was paraded in my face. In addition to conditions already related, I was often a witness to both parents' inappropriate behavior.

We were very small, for instance, when they told the three of us—Chuck, Mary, and me—to sleep in their bedroom on the second floor. In order to get to the bathroom, we had to walk through a small bedroom. In that bedroom was a visiting sailor, whom they called their cousin, and a married woman, whose husband and three children were at home, while she was there in the bed with our so-called cousin.

On more than one occasion, I saw my mother in the back of a car in a very compromising way with our neighbor's husband. So letting Ron make love to me didn't seem inappropriate at all. As a matter of fact, I thought that was what I was supposed to do.

Ron had my consent. What I had to put up with from my mother's husband was assault, which I was forced into through aggression and mind control. I hated him! I was deeply repulsed and scarred emotionally by his vulgar, inexcusable behavior.

My entire childhood was one of slavery. I lived as though I were in prison. I had freedom to go to school, be with friends, and drive the car. These activities, which were natural and normal for my friends, were freedoms for me only if I did exactly as I was told.

As an adult reflecting back on the confusion of those events, I realized Chuck was having the same experience. Unless we followed dad's agenda, our activities would be restricted, and we would be beaten. Sometimes it only took seeing a three-inch leather razor strap in his hands, or being forced to watch while he beat our mother, to realize exactly his intent.

It was 1947 and time for Ron to graduate. He was off to the University of Southern California to major in medicine. The last time I saw him he told me our relationship was over. He said, "I don't really love you!" I cried uncontrollably. I guess he felt so bad that he asked me out again that evening. We had an even better time than we had before, which left me even more confused.

I tried to reach him by phone the next day, but he was nowhere to be found. Though I asked his mother to tell him I'd called, he never returned my call. He literally broke my heart. It would be years before I could imagine my life without him.

On a Sunday afternoon after returning to the South Bay to start my junior year at RUHS, I saw two men walking along the Hermosa Beach strand. Ron was one of them. I walked toward him. Though our eyes met, he walked right by.

When you love someone with as much neediness as I loved Ron, it is so difficult to see that person again without extreme emotion and pain. This further convinced me he had absolutely no feelings for me.

I felt so poorly about myself! I wanted desperately to know love, and he made me feel that safety and emotion. I was terribly ignorant and confused regarding all acceptable behavior. I didn't know that sexual involvement during the teen years was inappropriate and destructive. I couldn't understand why we broke up and was extremely depressed.

Sometime later that summer, I ran into him a second time when leaving a movie theater in Redondo Beach. This time he followed me to the car where we talked senselessly for a short time and hugged one another. Neither of us could discuss our real feelings. Obviously we didn't understand them nor did we have the wisdom to try to sort through them.

By that time, I was seeing someone else. When I told Ron, he became angry, and we parted again.

It's amazing how many times we ran into one another. I realized while writing about these events that those occasions were opportunities to discuss our feelings. Because of our inability to communicate, however, we didn't get back together again. I knew I loved Ron, but I was convinced that those feelings were not reciprocal.

While sitting in a car waiting for a friend who had stopped by USC to pick up some books, I saw Ron again. He was walking in the direction of my parked car and stopped a few yards away, under the shade of a magnolia tree. He appeared to be waiting for someone. He had an orange in his hand. He glanced right at me. For a moment, I thought he noticed me, although he acted as if he hadn't.

Looking back, I realized a reflection on the window could have prevented him from seeing who it was sitting in the car looking longingly at him. Or, perhaps I reasoned at the time, this might be another occasion when he would recognize me and pass right by. In any case, I didn't want to be confronted with rejection again, so I never got out of the car to talk to him, which was a huge mistake!

I've since learned that teenage girls often experience sexual activity when they haven't had the advantage of a loving father figure in their developing years. It takes a dad who exhibits an active interest in his daughter's life, a father she can approach and trust, a dad with whom she can communicate. It takes a father who is present—mentally, physically, and spiritually. A loving father shows a profound interest in his daughter's life and her activities. He relates to her in a way that encourages her to share her thoughts and concerns. A dialogue between parent and offspring must exist. It is a developing need and imperative lesson of trust.

If a young woman doesn't have these basic needs met by her father while growing up, and if she becomes sexually active, she is trying to satisfy an obvious need for love, understanding, and male connection.

Dr. Phil says, "If a parent sends a child out of the house thirsty, the child will look for water wherever she can find it."

When I met Ron I was looking for the proverbial cup of cold water. For approximately two years he met that thirst. He met it by giving me a glimpse of what it meant to love and trust.

I later learned that morality is a state of consciousness, and if a teenager hasn't had the good fortune of learning through parental guidance the importance of abstinence, morality can be learned and demonstrated through education and spiritual growth.

Because of betrayal by an adult, it is impossible for a violated child to judge people well. They can't even trust their own judgment. Even minimal violation leaves the victim with shame, suicidal thoughts, and depression.

I knew far too much about the dark side of life and way too little about feelings of safety, comfort, wholesomeness, and inner peace, and yet I had a heart of innocence.

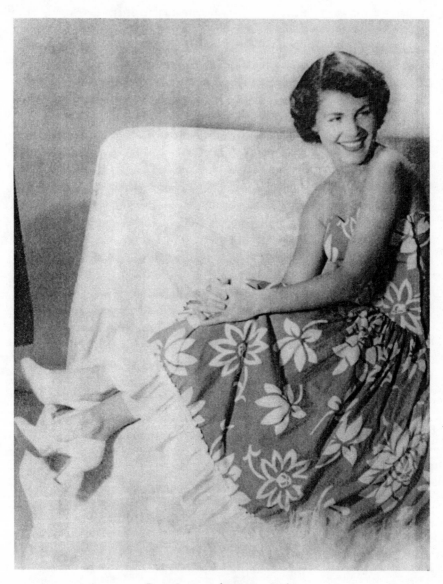

BettyJo at eighteen in 1949

Ron in the early 1950s

We Become What We Believe

Creating Ourselves

It is my absolute conviction that the most precious experience one can have here on earth is the good fortune of being raised by devoted, wise, and loving parents. Unfortunately, for many that isn't the case. So, the question arises, what happens to children who've experienced an abusive, unloving home? How do they survive? Sadly, I'll tell you about two who didn't.

As a little girl, my sister, Mary Elizabeth, was exquisite! Her blonde hair, dimples, and Shirley Temple-like curls often caused people to turn and stare. Like our grandmother, Mary had a beautiful nature and disposition. Throughout her life she exemplified gentleness. She laughed generously and wore a smiling expression from dawn to dusk. Before reaching her adult years, Mary learned to play the guitar and developed a beautiful singing voice.

Mother often told me I was mean and Mary was sweet. Actually, that was true. I was noticeably unhappy compared to my sister.

Charles Stanley, my brother, was eighteen months younger than I and eighteen months older than our sister. He had dark, wavy hair. He had a loving heart, and his smile was infectious. Like Mary, Chuck was gifted with a lovely voice.

As an industrious teenager, my brother rose early and worked every day for a local nursery before going to morning and afternoon classes at RUHS. He inherited a natural ability for horticulture from our grandfather, George

Edward Fondren. Before the age of fourteen, he earned his own spending money and contributed to the household.

By fourteen, I worked at J.C. Penny in Hermosa Beach weekdays after school, weekends, summers, and school vacations, and for the same purpose.

Mary and Chuck were very close. I wasn't as close to them as they were to one another. My desire to be separate from my parents also influenced my feelings toward my brother and sister. Sadly, I knew intuitively I wouldn't remain in their lives.

Oprah Winfrey wrote in her book *What I Know For Sure*: "I knew that my soul's survival depended on me. I felt I would have to fend for myself. I now think that the sense of being apart from others is what led me to trust so firmly in something bigger than I could articulate, and feel a connection to God." Oprah has defined exactly what I felt during my youth.

Though it wasn't fair of me to visualize myself separate from my siblings, it seemed natural—what I had to do. I realized that having them in my life was a constant reminder of our childhood.

While growing up, I believed I was the only child being abused. Though I wondered about Chuck and eventually realized he, too, experienced the same abuse, I didn't know Mary was summoned whenever I wasn't home or available.

During our childhood, my sister and I occasionally shared the same bedroom, and yet neither of us confided in the other. I was outraged for Mary when I eventually learned she had been molested, too. It was that rage that impelled me to go to the Hermosa Beach Police in '50, only to find zero support.

Had we told anyone at the time about what we were experiencing at home, our lives would have been more at risk, since not even the police could have protected us. The predator needed and depended on secrecy in order to carry out his aggressions. Making sure we were too frightened to speak even to one another was a method he used to guarantee success for his evil behavior.

If laws had been created earlier to protect children from sexual abuse, we would have had our day in court. Even if that had happened, because of his sense of love, I may have never been able to rely on Chuck to testify against our parents. Mary and I would have had to face the predators alone. I don't believe my brother had the moral courage to testify against mother. He may have been willing to do so against Charles Earl Root, but not against our mother.

There was a time when Chuck was growing up that he wanted to become a minister. After he married and realized no support for fulfilling that desire, his whole attitude toward life changed. He even stopped singing.

Thinking back on our childhood, especially how we lived in a perpetual state of fear and complete lack of wholesome love, I wonder how any of us made it to adulthood.

There was some welcome but unexpected support for me, however, after returning from Hemet to the South Bay. Ron, my high school sweetheart, started classes at USC the same year I returned from Hemet High to Redondo Union High School.

It was comforting to be back in Redondo Beach. Having attended the elementary school at Grant on Aviation and the sixth through eighth grades at Central, I knew a lot of people. Returning to the South Bay brought a new sense of hope for a more stable existence.

During my junior year, I tried out for song leader with a close friend, Beverly Hustead. We were both chosen. The wholesome attention and friendship we received from our peers was a welcome change.

At Redondo in the '40s, every girl wore a uniform. In addition to Student Council, we had Girls' Court. I was elected Girls' Judge and served on the council.

At the end of our senior football season, I was chosen Football Sweetheart. At the May Queen Ball, one of my best friends, Sally Masury, was elected Queen. Beverly Hustead was Second Princess, and I was First Princess. Sublimation wasn't a term I understood in those days, but it was an obvious occurrence in my life. Due to the abuse that was continuing at home, however, I remained extremely depressed. One day when the sadness was more aggressive than usual, I went to the Girls' Vice Principal's Office to see Miss Rous. I was in a state of paranoia, completely out of control. She asked me what was wrong. All I could say was, "No one likes me!" She asked, "Why do you feel that way?"

I couldn't tell her that I had no dignity, no sense of worth, and all I felt was shame. All I could do was cry. Finally, after I said, "No one likes me" for the third or forth time, she remarked, "It's strange you say that, because the difference in votes between May Queen and First Princess is one vote."

These activities eventually helped me begin to realize that I was liked. Up to that point, I had spent my entire life thinking I was incapable of receiving any good and that no one I cared about cared for me in return. These events showed me that love—a presence beyond that of self—was present whether I recognized it or not.

After we returned to the South Bay, my parents enrolled me in modeling school and acting classes. Both activities took me to Beverly Hills once a week. And, without consulting me, they entered me in a beauty pageant in Long Beach.

A second-place position in the brunette category was the result. Again without my knowledge, my parents rushed my bathing suit photo to the *Daily Breeze*. After the picture appeared in the paper, I was even more humiliated. All I felt was shame.

It was a good thing after all, for as a result of the contest, I did a remarkable thing. I told my parents I would no longer go to modeling school or take acting classes. I explained I had no interest in being placed in the position of parading before people. And, I said, "You can't force me to do it!"

Much to my surprise they didn't, but they started right in on my sister, Mary. They subjected her to very suggestive photographs. Their long-term goal and desire to use us was based on illusions of grandeur. They wanted to place one of us in the movies. They received a rejection letter from Mary Pickford—Canadian movie actress, co-founder of United Artists, and one of 36 founders of the Academy of Motion Picture Arts and Sciences—in response to one of their inquiries.

On graduation day for the class of '49, E.T. gave me a surprising gift. She finally told me she had been married twice, and that Doyle James Byrd was my real father.

She also explained that when she divorced Doyle, she learned through her attorney that his name wasn't correctly spelled on their marriage license, but she gave me no reason for the misspelling. His true name was Doyle James Bird.

I was furious at her for not telling me sooner. I felt cheated and outraged. At the same time, I was relieved. I thanked God I wasn't related to her second husband. That was a fact I intuitively felt throughout my youth. My younger brother, Chuck, wasn't his child either. My sister, Mary, was his daughter, however.

Though I was forced to live my entire youth by the predator's name, my maiden name was really Byrd (or Bird). When I needed a passport several years later, my birth certificate confirmed this fact.

The day after high school graduation, I started my first job in the field of dentistry. A few days later and with the support of a roommate, Jackie Singletary, I moved to the Surf Apartments on the ocean—the south side of the pier in Manhattan Beach.

Once I moved, I seldom saw Mary or Chuck. To this day I regret abandoning them. They deserved a sister's friendship, love, and support. Failing them was an example of the cold person I had become.

Though Oprah's statement makes incredible sense to me today, at the time I felt only guilt for not being present for Mary and Chuck. I knew I had to move on, but I didn't fully understand the wisdom of separating myself from family.

I was nineteen before Mary told me she was experiencing the same abuse. She came to see me after I moved from my first apartment in Manhattan Beach to Hermosa Beach. Mary wanted to get away from her dad. It was her testimony in '50 that gave me the courage to go to the police and tell them our story.

The police should have been able to help me get Mary out of the house. They let me pour out all the painful details. After listening to the entire story, they said, "We're sorry, but there is nothing we can do. A man's home is his castle."

I was shocked! I needed to get my sister away from her dad, but I had no support from anyone, not even the police. Going to mother wasn't an option. She was part of the problem.

The only thing I could think of doing was to arrange for Mary to leave the South Bay and move away where our parents couldn't find her. So I made arrangements to send Mary to Hemet, where she could live with a family we knew there.

Unfortunately that didn't turn out well because they had a son, and Mary became pregnant. Sadly, she came to me wanting an abortion. A facility was somehow found for her.

Around this time, I started thinking more deeply about each of our lives. I had assumed that I was the only one experiencing abuse. The truth is that the pedophile was dragging all three of us through the nightmare during our entire childhood.

Strange, inexplicable occurrences were going on. Sometime, when I was between the ages of ten and twelve, two men frequently came to our home. One had bleached blonde hair, which was rare for men in the early '40s. One of them played the piano while the other disappeared with my stepdad and brother.

Chuck's room was over the garage. The only way to enter or leave his room was from an outside stairway. I hate to think what was going on there. The household predator was apparently bisexual. If he wasn't violating me, or my sister, he presumably was forcing himself on my brother.

It's hard to believe that I grew up without being conscious of what the other two were subjected to. The fact that we were conditioned by the beatings we experienced or witnessed led me to the realization that our lives are completely subjective. We only see what we are willing to see. Fear kept each of us in a state of mind control.

Children in immense pain and shame often conceal their emotions and cover up their feelings. If they feel they won't be believed, they refrain from revealing their fears or problems to one another, or to an adult.

In the exhaustion of living in our own adversity, we fail to see what is taking place in the lives of those around us. Though I was never able to prove my adult suspicions regarding my brother, I believe he may have mirrored bisexual tendencies as a result of being sexually molested by our stepdad. My fear, however, may be supposition rather than fact.

What caused this fear were the several strange conversations we had on the phone before Chuck passed on. He tried to tell me many things. At that time, I wasn't ready to face my suspicions about what might have been done to him, nor was I ready to discuss the past.

Since his death, remarks by other members of the family and mentally sorting through our childhood experiences reinforced my fear.

Unfortunately, Chuck and Mary were both gone before laws were put into place that would have enabled us to bring the child molester (or molesters) to court.

Though we rarely communicated our feelings for one another, I loved my brother and sister deeply. Their beauty and innocence remain with me even today.

As a high school dropout, Mary seemed to have learning disabilities—a problem grossly misunderstood in the '40s. She was attractive, loving, and very bright. Mary never lacked intelligence.

Like our brother, she had a wonderfully warm heart. And unlike the rest of us, Mary had a predilection for laughter.

I believe the reason I've been determined to live a full life has been an insatiable desire for an existence apart from the example I was shown. I no longer think it's unusual that I grew up with an inexplicable contempt for iniquity. I've come to the realization that the feelings I felt for the way we were used in our childhood were normal and healthy.

Repulsion for both parents engrained a profound message in my heart. There wasn't a single facet of their chosen lifestyle I wanted to mirror in my own existence. I had lived with a deep-seated feeling all my youth that I was an observer of my family and not a participant.

When one grows up in that kind of environment, however, behavioral flaws are deeply engrained in one's character whether or not one has become addicted to drugs, alcohol, or a parental lifestyle. Fortunately, I was never attracted to or mesmerized by any of their habits or actions.

I had so much to overcome in the way of anger and coldness, however. One doesn't have to be a slave to alcohol and drugs in order to adopt behavioral dysfunction. Dysfunction is insidious, and like so many habits, it can be a mirrored pattern of behavior. If one has never been shown how to express warmth and tenderness, even making friends can remain a mystery.

This type of attitude seems to continue until one has the resolve to grow spiritually. Doing nothing is always less frightening than instigating change. Without humility and the willingness to change, one can miss out on the blessings derived from healing. Spiritual healing is indeed the solution to any and all adversity.

Occasionally, I find myself reverting to feelings of grief. I've had to consciously make a distinction between the thoughts I want to own and those I choose to discard in order to be present in the moment and feel the freedom and peace I know is possible. Wisdom has carefully guided me through a constant selection of thoughts.

Chuck became a bank president. He left California in the mid-'60s and moved to Oregon. Several years later something terrible happened there because he left his job as bank president and disappeared for three or four months. No one could find him or knew where he was.

He called me a couple of times before he suddenly disappeared. He was terribly distraught. He gave no clue as to what was troubling him. Discussing the past with my brother was impossible, because I was still unwilling to face my own issues with what had happened. It was only a few months later when I received a call informing me that soon after Chuck returned home he died.

Chuck passed on in '67 at the age of thirty-four. He had been separated from his wife. After mysteriously leaving his job and disappearing for three months, Chuck returned home one morning around 6 a.m. His wife saw him drive up the driveway and pull into the garage. Expecting he would walk in the house, she waited. He didn't come right in, so she started doing some chores thinking he might be talking to a neighbor or just taking his time to remove his things from the car.

When she started looking for him, to her amazement, he was still in the garage. The garage door was shut. The car was still running, and the driver's window was rolled down. Chuck's body was resting against the driver's seat. He was dead. The coroner pronounced his death as an accidental suicide, but we all knew he had taken his own life.

My brother had an awareness, sensitivity, and inner kindness beyond his years. He was deeply intuitive and thoughtfully loving. He didn't deserve to pass on at such an early age. The fact that he did was just one more example of how devastating it can be to an adult not to have the foundation and nourishment of a wholesome childhood.

Tremendous strength is needed to face life one day at a time, and a stable childhood prepares one for life's challenges. The adversities of my dear brother's life were obviously anything but useful or sweet to him.

Chuck's death was a huge loss. All the things I might have done to help him ran through my thoughts over and over again. It was too late! I wasn't there for my brother and there would never be another opportunity. If I had been less selfish with my own feelings, I would have gone to him when he called me just before his disappearance. I still think of Chuck almost every day.

Not long after Chuck's funeral, I invited my sister and mother to our home in Pebble Beach. It was the first time in many years I felt comfortable enough to attempt to reach out to them.

During the mid-'40s (WWII), my mother worked for the FBI. It was her job to manage the internment of several Japanese families. The Japanese lived in a trailer park in Redondo Beach, which had a wire fence completely around the camp.

Years later, Ethel wanted to visit some of the interned who had remained her friends. So my husband, JP, and I decided to drive my sister and mother to Southern California to the home of one of her friends for a visit.

On the way there, and for the first time, I revealed the thoughts that had occurred to me when I was a child in the hospital with polio and while being treated for third degree burns five years later.

Ethel was surprised. She had no idea I'd had such thoughts. Her remark was, "You're a healer, just like your grandmother."

Another interesting realization occurred while visiting her Japanese friends. The younger of the women looked at my husband and said, "You were our abalone man!" For a moment, JP looked back at her in confusion, and then he suddenly remembered.

During the time of Japanese internment, he dove for abalone off the coast of Redondo and Palos Verdes and brought his catch to the camp to sell. After more than thirty years, he was recognized.

By the time my sister was in her forties, she had been married several times. She was the mother of three children. Just before she married for the final time, she moved to Carmel. She found a job as manager of a bed and breakfast inn called Happy Landing. Whenever she answered the phone, she sounded genuinely happy.

Before Mary remarried and moved away, we became a little closer. I didn't reveal too much of the sister I'm sure she needed to know, as I was unaware of being cold and unapproachable.

Mary was fascinated with the healings that had occurred in my life. She attended church with me, since it was right next door to her work place.

Not long after, she moved to Southern California. I had no idea, nor did she, when she moved to Carmel that she had lung cancer. Mary was a chain smoker. She was a jewel layered with years of unnecessary pain. Through all that, she, like our grandmother, was an exquisite example of pure love.

So many times I tried to find a way to tell my high school teachers, the vice principals, the counselors what was happening at home. I could never bring myself to speak the words. If I had told them, what would have happened to us? Since the police couldn't have protected us, our lives would have been in further jeopardy if I had told someone. Life was full of denial caused by deep-seated fear and trauma. It was a life completely deprived of communication. All feelings were suppressed.

When the past ceases to overshadow the joy of our present moments, then, and only then, are we free to soar above what would otherwise be dreadful memories.

To achieve dominion over a tragic past, I had to lose myself materially to find myself spiritually. I had a choice. I could continue to accept the negative, depressing thoughts nudging at me or I could turn from them and adopt a higher viewpoint. I chose the option of looking beyond self. Without ignoring my feelings, I used them as a springboard to adopt a higher level of thought and action.

Mindful Loving by Henry Grayson, PhD, states, "It is the negative thoughts that we have to be most watchful of, for these are evidence of the ego at work. . . . As long as we think the thoughts we have always thought, with the frequency with which we have thought them, and as unconsciously, our lives and our relationships can never consistently improve, for we will be imprisoned in the ego mind's way of thinking. Until we become the master of our minds, we cannot take charge of our feelings and our relationships, and we will experience ourselves as being at the effect of others—essentially an experience of victimization."

Grayson writes further, "Powerless and critical thoughts bring depression. . . . Failure or worthless thoughts bring failure; rejection thoughts invite rejection, comparative and judging thoughts make us miserable, jealous thoughts make us anxious and depressed, and the list goes on."

As adults, we have the reasoning ability and the power to recreate, revise our lives on a level of thinking that transcends fear or limited, material sense. We need affirmations of good, of peace and dominion. We need to understand how very precious we are. Our innate innocence, dignity, and goodness remain unscathed by anything or anyone. It is our natural heritage and remains within, waiting to be claimed.

Don Miguel Ruiz writes in *The Mastery of Love*, "You have the power to create. Your power is so strong that whatever you believe comes true. You create yourself, whatever you believe you are. You are the way you are because that is what you believe about yourself. Your whole reality, everything you believe, is your creation. You have the same power as any other human in the world. The main difference between you and someone else is how you apply your power, what you create with your power."

The Bible reads, "As a man thinketh in his heart, so is he." James Allen, in his book, *As a Man Thinketh*, insists on the possibility of man to mold his own character and create his own happiness. He believed in man's innate goodness and divine rationality. He wrote, "All that we are is the result of what we've thought. A man can only rise, conquer and achieve by lifting up his thoughts. Today we are where our thoughts have taken us, and we are the architects—for better or worse—of our future. A man is literally what he thinks. His character is the sum of all his thoughts."

Mary Elizabeth Root in the 1940s

Charles Stanley Root in 1952

Surviving Child Abuse

One Out of Every Four Children is a Victim

What I observed from a childhood of exposure to a serial predator, my stepfather, Charles Earl Root, is that he was fully aware of his actions. He consciously chose to listen to his own sensual thoughts and act out his criminal impulses. Responsibility for crimes he committed against me, my sister, and perhaps my brother wasn't of the least concern to him.

Control over a child's ability to think independently and to act out of his own spirit is the goal of the pedophile. He attempts to destroy a child's dignity and sense of worth for his own evil, selfish gain, and addiction to lust and power. He'll make dreadful threats to gain complete control of the mind of his chosen prey.

Once the pedophile's goal is achieved, the child lives according to the will of the predator. This leaves the victim in a chronic state of fearing the loss of his own life, the life of a parent, or members of his immediate family.

Shawn Hornbeck was kidnapped by Michael Devlin in October of 2002. Shawn was eleven years old.

After holding Shawn captive for a month, Devlin told Shawn he was taking him home. Instead he drove him from a suburb of St. Louis, Missouri, to a remote logging road near Shawn's home in Washington County, Missouri, where he attempted to smother his victim. Shawn begged for his life. He promised Devlin that if he would spare him, he would stay with Devlin and do whatever he asked.

From then on, Shawn was so under Devlin's mental control that he passed up an opportunity to reveal himself to the local police when they stopped him and a friend for bicycling after curfew one night.

Another time, he specifically denied who he was when asked by his friend's mother. After seeing a photograph of Shawn Hornbeck on the television news, she asked him if that was he. He laughed, said, "No," and then added as teenagers often do, "Whatever."

He had the opportunity to reveal himself to her. But he didn't. Shawn's reluctance to seize the moment and reveal his true identity is an example of how a pedophile's threat to harm or kill a child can make a child totally subservient.

It's the fear of loss of one's own life or the lives of one's family members that keeps the victim under the will of the predator.

For over four years, Shawn was mesmerized by fear. After the first month of his captivity, he had freedom everyday to pick up the phone to call his parents, or walk into a police station to expose the pedophile, and yet, he waited.

While searching for another kidnap victim, the police accidentally found Shawn in January 2007. Shawn writes on his website: "I prayed everyday that my parents would find me."

I know full well why Shawn remained verbally paralyzed by the hideous events of his kidnapping. I lived with my brother and sister under the same roof until I was eighteen, yet we never discussed what was going on with us individually. If we had, we knew full well what would happen to us and might happen to our mother. Victims are frozen in an emotional psyche of helplessness.

On October 9, 2007, Shawn's attorney revealed on television that Michael Devlin, Shawn's predator, pleaded guilty to the fact that he kidnapped, raped and tried to kill Shawn.

I've spent most of my life in a state of posttraumatic numbness. To become the balanced person I longed to be, dominion over the past and discipline of thought became my primary goal. Feelings of lack of dignity and worthiness have made me determined to prevail mentally and physically.

Oprah shares the wisdom of the following statement in her book, *What I Know For Sure*: "One of the most important challenges of your life is to heal the wounds of your past so you don't continue to bleed. Until you do, you are literally dragging the weight of your past into your present. And that makes it nearly impossible to move forward."

Secrecy is one of the most powerful tools a predator uses in victimizing children. Until the development of the Internet, most predators were people known personally to their victims.

Statistics prove that the vast majority of criminals who sexually assault children have not been cured and most likely will repeat their crimes.

When children exposed to this insanity enter adulthood, society risks the possibility of their repeating the offenses that were inflicted on them. Aristotle wrote, "We are what we repeatedly do."

It's been estimated that predators will molest on the average of 117 children before they are discovered and exposed. And it's been reported that over five hundred thousand sexual predators live in the United States. According to John Walsh, host of the television program *America's Most Wanted* and a child protection advocate, this figure represents only *the known offenders, and only 1 percent of those known have ever been arrested.*

If it is true that known predators molest on average 117 children before they are arrested, then many millions of children have been victimized.

Society can best protect children from pedophiles by incarcerating them. Imprisoning a person who has no control over his/her selfish behavior is doing the public a service. "It is in justice that the ordering of society is centered," wrote Aristotle.

If a predator seeks reformation of thought, is genuinely remorseful for indulging his own sensuousness at the expense of the helpless and innocent, and if he follows through by changing and purifying his behavior, he *may* experience regeneration of character.

On the other hand, if he shows no practical repentance, the pedophile will continue his lifestyle at the expense of the innocent. If evil is not rebuked in his thought, it will continue to nurture itself. Prison then may be the best place for him and a force for inward reflection.

It's been proven, however, that few, if any, feel genuine remorse. Most repeat their dreadful ways and are unwilling to change their way of life.

A quotation by an English poet, Nicholas Rowe, in *The New Dictionary of Thoughts*—an encyclopedia of quotations—is relevant: "Conscious remorse and anguish must be felt, to curb desire, to break the stubborn will, and work a second nature in the soul, ere virtue can regain the place she lost."

When one seeks genuine repentance and no longer is tempted by evil suggestions, when addictions are faced and ended, when inappropriate behavior is purified and forsaken, a sinful past can be forgiven.

No state should adopt statutes of limitations, since it can take some victims a long time to find the moral courage necessary to expose a pedophile. Regardless of age or time, nothing should prevent predators from being exposed by their victims.

Persons who remain in denial of such crimes contribute to the problem and actually help further child abuse. Why do we as a nation allow this insanity to continue? Children should never have to grow up fearing for their safety.

The Roman Catholic priest, peace activist, and poet, Father Daniel Berrigan, said: "I don't know a more irreligious attitude, one more utterly bankrupt of any human content, than one which permits children to be destroyed."

Sexual exploitation of children through the use of the Internet is growing dramatically. "Over the past four years, the number of reports of child pornography sites to the National Center for Missing & Exploited children (NCMEC) has grown by almost 400 percent." (*Christian Science Monitor*, August 18, 2005).

Children are spending more and more time online. Seventy-five percent of all teenagers search and use the Internet. Protecting them while they are at their computers has reached a state of emergency.

The October 18, 2006, *Wall Street Journal* article by Jessica Vascellaro and Anjali Athavaley states that one in seven ten- to fourteen-year-olds who use the Internet have received a sexual solicitation online. The article listed new software a parent can install that sends the parent a warning when sexual or predatory language appears in children's Instant Messaging conversations. It is the IMSafer program.

The same article listed additional software that allows parents to monitor children's computer use. These are Solid Oak Software Inc.'s, CYBERsitter, a Web filtering tool, and a social networking profile tracker from BeNetSafe LLC. SearchHelp Inc. of Syosset, N.Y., has a software program that allows parents to block websites, look at kids' computers in real time, and receive text messages or e-mails when their children type or search for certain keywords and suspicious phrases, phone numbers, etc.

Internet Safety by John Walsh is an imperative book for parents. Walsh and Julie Clark have teamed up to create a website for the safety of children, which is www.thesafeside.com.

John Hughes, former editor of the *Desert Morning News,* wrote in the Aug. 16, 2006, edition of *The Christian Science Monitor* the following: "It should not require a doctorate in psychology to understand that what we see and hear can influence our behavior." Hughes also quoted Judith Reisman, author of *"The Psycho-pharmacology of Pictorial Pornography,"* as saying she sees a direct link between pornography and sex crimes. Reisman further says: "It's not that pornography acts like a drug. It is a drug." Most [if not all] convicted sexual predators share an addiction to porn.

New Mexico is the first state to express moral courage in its handling of pedophiles. Sexual predators in New Mexico now receive life in prison.

In an attempt to deal with pain, it's not unusual for abused children to develop addictions to alcohol, drugs, porn, and prostitution. A lack of worth, value, and love for one's self can lead to these destructive and often fatal lifestyles.

The irony of our justice system is that if one has HIV and knowingly infects one or more persons, he/she can be imprisoned for up to one hundred and eighty years. By comparison, the courts hold sexual predators for a relatively short period of time.

All lawmakers—assemblymen, state and federal senators, members of the House of Representatives—are at fault. It is their *duty* to create laws to protect the innocent. It is the inalienable right of every American to be free. Protection from predators should be a child's primary right.

To free pedophiles from prison is a decision against the human rights of innocent children! Winston Churchill wrote, "There is no virtue in a tame acquiescence in evil. To protest against cruelty and wrong, and to strive to end them, is the mark of a man." Lawmakers and sentencing judges should get this message and get it quickly. Pedophiles should be anathematized from society. According to Shakespeare, "Action is eloquence."

On July 19, 2006, USC's Director of the Gene Therapy Department, William French Anderson—a graduate of Harvard College (1958) and Harvard Medical School (1963)—was convicted of child molestation charges. Referred to as the "Father of Gene Therapy" and runner-up for *Time* magazine's choice of "Man of the Year" in 1995, Anderson was convicted of one count of continuous sexual abuse of a child under the age of fourteen and three counts of committing a lewd act upon a child beginning in 1997 over a four-year period at his Los Angeles home. He was sentenced to prison for fourteen years. Anderson had previously been charged with sexually molesting a twelve-year-old boy in Montgomery County, Maryland, between 1983 and 1985. Prosecutors dropped the charges, citing insufficient evidence under Maryland law.

Thinking they are protecting their victimized child from further emotional trauma, many parents have refused to press charges. Though their parental decision is understandable, it may be that by refusing to face the predator, closure for the child is prolonged or possibly lost. Their decision could also free the criminal to molest again.

I saw my predator accidentally for the last time in 1956 when I was twenty-five. He told me he was dying of cancer. I was totally unconcerned about his condition. I blurted out, "Why did you do that to us?" His reply was quick, purely debased, and selfish. He said, "I thought that's why God gave me children."

I was repulsed and deeply saddened by his answer and totally unprepared to confront him further. I wanted desperately to tell him how much harm his cruel, selfish acts had caused. If I had been emotionally prepared to confront him fully, I believe I could have realized a path of healing much earlier.

On May 16, 2005, television news revealed that eight-year-old Shasta Groene and her nine-year-old brother, Dylan, were missing from their Idaho home.

On July 2nd, Shasta was found in a restaurant with a registered sex offender, Joseph Edward Duncan III. There was an outstanding warrant against Duncan for failing to register as a sex offender with a criminal history of rape.

Pedophiles will also murder in order to seize their victims. Shasta and Dylan's older brother, mother, and their mother's fiancé were bludgeoned to death at the same time Shasta and Dylan were kidnapped. When Shasta was found, Dylan wasn't with her and was feared dead. Sadly, a television update on July 11, 2005, revealed that Dylan's remains were found in Montana.

Jessica Lunsford's kidnapping from her Florida bedroom by a pedophile, John Evander Couey, who lived one hundred and fifty yards from Jessica, was on the news continuously in February of 2005. On March 18th, Jessica's body was found under Couey's back porch. He had raped nine-year-old Jessica and buried her alive. Couey's known history of pedophilia dated back twenty-seven years to 1978.

Jessica's father, Mark Lunsford, has been tireless in his efforts to get states to pass Jessica's Law. He now serves as Chairman of the Advisory Board of Stop Child Predators. An update on Jessica's case revealed that on August 24, 2007, Couey was sentenced to death.

Jessica's Law—a 2005 Florida law that has been the basis for similar legislation in other states—is designed to punish sex offenders and reduce their ability to molest or rape again. It imposes more stringent tracking of released offenders.

Dean Arthur Schwartzmiller—a serial predator—focused on befriending parents to gain access to their children. After gaining parents' trust, he molested their children. Once exposed, he failed to register as a sex offender.

According to NBC's *Dateline*, each time Schwartzmiller was found by police, he managed to flee from one state to another. When caught, he'd jump bail; when taken to court, he would attack his victims; when convicted, his convictions were overturned on appeal. Schwartzmiller spent years avoiding arrest and prosecution by manipulating the courts that released him on nine separate occasions.

He continued to get away until his arrest in Everett, Washington, in May 2005. At that time, police confiscated several notebooks containing one thousand and five hundred pages of thousands of names of children with specific details of sexual crimes committed against them. With at least thirty-six thousand entries in the notebooks, it has been assumed that a number of them referred to boys he desired or imagined. But the notebooks show his huge appetite for sexually abusing children, and his criminal record shows that he acted on that appetite numerous times.

Schwartzmiller's molestation charges dated back to 1970 when he was first arrested in Juneau, Alaska. He has been labeled by *Dateline* as the worst of child molesters. His criminal history is recorded in six states and occurred over thirty years.

On January 29, 2007, Schwartzmiller was sentenced to one hundred and fifty-two years in prison for abusing two twelve-year-old boys. He was given the maximum term on eleven felony counts of child molestation and one misdemeanor charge of child pornography possession.

On May 25, 2005, CBS' "*60 Minutes*" reported how in 1991 five men came forward to charge that Father Richard Lavigne, a priest in the Catholic diocese of Springfield, Massachusetts, had sexually abused them when they were boys. More came forward, until a total of forty-three men all charged that Lavigne had abused them as children.

On December 4, 2003, *The Boston Glob*, reported that "in 1994 the diocese paid $1.4 million to settle claims brought by 17 people who said Lavigne abused them, and Lavigne now faces another 20 claims."

According to *60 Minutes*, Father Richard Lavigne has been the prime suspect for decades in the 1972 murder of thirteen-year-old Danny Croteau, who had been one of Lavigne's altar boys.

Danny's friend, Tom Martin, said that Danny told him that he hated Lavigne and that Lavigne had hurt him. Martin believed Danny meant that Lavigne had sexually abused him, because Martin said that he himself had been sexually abused by Lavigne on two occasions. Evidence pointing to Lavigne in the murder of Croteau is circumstantial, so there has never been a trial, but former State Detective, Ed Harrington, said that Lavigne was the only suspect he was ever aware of and that was ever investigated. Lavigne has claimed that he has evidence that exonerates him.

Richard Lavigne has been removed from his status as a priest within the Catholic Church. Lavigne—no longer Father Lavigne—still lives in Springfield.

The Washington Post reported on September 28, 2004 that Bishop Thomas Dupre, once head of the Springfield, Massachusetts, Roman Catholic Diocese, was indicted on two counts of child rape, allegedly committed when he was a priest. But he was not prosecuted because the statue of limitations on the case had expired. He was admitted earlier that year to the St. Luke's Institute in Silver Spring, Maryland, where Catholic clergy are treated for pedophilia, among other disorders.

Michael Patrick Driscoll served as chancellor and later as auxiliary bishop of the Roman Catholic Church in Orange County, California, from 1976 to 1999. He moved to Boise, Idaho, to serve as bishop of the Diocese of Boise. Driscoll moved priests accused of molesting minors from parish to parish in Orange County. According to the *Orange County Register*, he helped priests relocate to other dioceses and countries to avoid prosecution and ignored or delayed acting on parents' complaints.

The Orange County Edition of the *Los Angeles Times* on Wednesday, May 26, 2005, published a lengthy article titled, *"Reports Show Failure of Therapy for Priests."* The article relates that in each of the nine cases cited, all efforts failed to rehabilitate the priests, who were known predators.

In July 2006, John Walsh celebrated the signing of the *Adam Walsh Children's Safety Act* and stated during his television conference that there are ten thousand Catholic priests who are pedophiles. Why aren't these priests subject to arrest like any other pedophiles? A number have simply been moved to a different parish.

On July 15, 2007, the *Los Angeles Times* reported that the Roman Catholic Archdiocese of Los Angeles agreed to pay six hundred and sixty million dollars to settle sexual abuse cases. Cardinal Roger Mahony publicly apologized to more than five hundred plaintiffs who each received an average of one million three hundred thousand dollars in the settlement.

No apology can possibly heal or erase the terror caused by molestation. No amount of money can give a victim the dignity he deserves, remove the flashbacks, or make the painful memories go away.

I know there are many good Catholic priests and lay people. They are not the problem. The problem is any individual or institution that covers up crime.

The church (any church) is where pedophiles often hide because it is the last place the public expects to find them. My stepfather was a minister before he married my mother.

Predators exist in all walks of life. Pedophilia doesn't exist just among the lustful uneducated. It also exists in the lives of the educated. Predators have included teachers, parents, ministers, stepparents, brothers, sisters, neighbors, relatives, doctors, priests, rabbis, and friends.

Sexual misconduct plaguing schools has been a recent subject of interest for *Associated Press*. An October 20, 2007, article by Martha Irvine and Robert Tanner revealed that an AP investigation "found more than two thousand and five hundred cases over five years in which educators were punished for actions from bizarre to sadistic." The article goes on to say, "Students in American schools are groped. They're raped. They're pursued and seduced and think they're in love. . . . And no one—not the schools, not the courts, not the state or federal governments—has found a surefire way to keep molesting teachers out of classrooms." Isn't this an area where specific laws of protection should be in place for children?

The newly established 2007 *Adam Walsh Children's Safety* Act demands all known predators be registered. Essentially the act gives the U.S. Attorney General the authority to apply the law retroactively; it establishes a national DNA database; increases the mandatory minimum incarceration period to twenty-five years for kidnapping or maiming a child and thirty years for having sex with a child younger than twelve or for sexually assaulting a child between thirteen and seventeen years of age; creates a National Child Abuse Registry to protect children from being adopted by convicted child abusers; and increases penalties for sex trafficking of children and child prostitution.

Sadly, it's been estimated on television news that *California has one predator for every two square miles.* If that number is correct, over *77 thousand pedophiles* exist in the state of California.

When I was a child, there were fewer pedophiles. In 2004, when this chapter was first being researched, information available on the Internet stated that one girl out of four and one boy out of six has experienced these crippling events.

However, Oprah quoted *one out of every four children* on her television program on January 13, 2006. We will continue to see these percentages increase until our lawmakers and courts enforce laws of protection for all children.

I know for a fact that Charles Earl Root, a known serial predator, came from a family of molesters. It took only one occasion of being left alone with his father to know that he, too, was a pedophile.

Though I've had my suspicions, I have no proof that my stepparent molested children outside of our immediate family. What leads me to suspect that he may have molested others was the fact that while I was still living at home two young boys—one at a time—lived with us. Knowing what he did to me and my sister and possibly my brother, has led me to be concerned for them.

Experience, and the need for healing, has led me to several conclusions. Generically speaking, man's spiritual (true) identity is always intact, untouched and separate from the corruption of the mortal, ego senses, whether they take the form of another's malicious action or one's own sense of despair due to dwelling on the past. Understanding this spiritual fact enables one to rediscover his dignity and facilitates the healing process.

To relive memories of the crime continues to give the predator power over you. Through spiritual growth one can demonstrate dominion in spite of past events, no matter how severe. This is the only process that frees one, and it does so from one's soul—the center of one's thoughts and feelings—outward.

I was deeply impressed years ago by the movie *Always*. Audrey Hepburn's remark to Richard Dreyfus was, "You can't gain freedom until you give freedom." Blame keeps the hurt alive. Wondering what we may have done as children to attract the pedophile is unnecessary, because invariably it was simply our being good, pure, innocent children that drew his attention.

The adult is the predator, and the condition is rape—rape of a child's dignity, innocence, and the demise of any possible self-esteem. This act destroys the wonders of childhood, forces the child into adulthood, crushes his/her dreams, and causes a lack of self-worth often followed by depression—deep depression, constant fear, and flashbacks of painful events.

Freedom begins when we stop blaming ourselves and cease blaming the predator. They are victims, too. They are victims of their own ignorance, the sensual thoughts they listen to, and evil actions they act upon. They are slaves to their addictions.

I've never been one to excuse people for their addictions. Though I've had compassion for the life they've wasted and the family they've disappointed, I know it's possible for people to change if they're sincerely willing to strive for a higher sense of humanity. So many hide behind their addictions and use them as a way of avoiding the work it takes to improve their character and become an asset to society.

Individual growth begins with changing our thought. Once a thought is changed for the better, lives begin to change.

Before an addiction is acted upon, thought presents itself as supposition or mental suggestion. It is at that moment that we can disown suggestion and declare it is not our thought but an evil suggestion and powerless to use us—our intelligence. Unless we choose to listen to suggestions and act upon them, they can't become a part of our experience.

A new view, free of blame, frees us to move beyond that of predator/victim and is an important step toward healing. This view alone may not always prevent a dreadful experience from rehearsing itself, but as we grow in our willingness to accept spiritual ideas, the prayerful work we do brings us the desired freedom and dominion over reoccurring flashbacks.

Through experience, I've learned that the sum of our human experience therefore is either the result of the sadness we feel from dwelling on the past or the wholesome goodness we choose to accept and claim as our thought and experience.

To arrive at the latter, one needs to learn to make a distinction between the material senses and spiritual sense. Whatever one chooses as reality becomes, or continues to be, one's experience.

We have a responsibility to ourselves, and our loved ones, to become whole regardless of the past. Nothing about the healing process is easy. The most difficult work we have to do is to change our thought and expectations about life. Finding dignity and peace enables us to act out that which presents the greatest and highest good for all concerned.

An article by Robert Langreth in *Forbes* magazine, April 2007, made the following statement regarding CBT, cognitive behavioral therapy: "Depression, anxiety and other ills aren't the cause of a cascade of debilitating thoughts and self loathing—they are, instead, a result of the same. Eliminate bad thoughts and you can short-circuit bad feelings. . . . Men are disturbed not by things but by the principles and notions which they form concerning things. . . . What you think has a powerful influence on symptoms."

James Allen wrote in his book, *As a Man Thinketh,* the following: "A man does not come to poverty or go to jail through the tyranny of fate or circumstance, but by the pathway of base thoughts and desires. Nor does a pure-minded man suddenly fall into crime by stress of external force. The criminal thought had long been secretly fostered in his heart, and the hour of his sin revealed its gathered power. Circumstance does not make the man; it reveals him to himself. No such conditions can exist in a man as vice and its attendant sufferings apart from vicious inclinations, or virtue and its pure happiness without the continued cultivation of virtuous aspirations."

From left to right: The visiting cousin, my mother, E.T., and the pedophile, Charles Earl Root

Naples, Long Beach to Carmel

Marriage

In 1951, at the age of twenty, I married for the first time. Within two years, I had my first child, a daughter named Shelley Anne. We were divorced in '55 when she was two.

On April 17, 1957, I married James Peter Cost. We met through mutual friends who attended RUHS and graduated with JP in '41.

He was a teacher in the Los Angeles secondary school system. JP taught art, set design, English, and math for several years at Narbonne High School in Harbor City. As an aspiring vice principal, he shared an office with three other would-be administrators. What was remarkable about this fact was that their names were Cost, Price, Sell, and Cheatum.

During his undergraduate years at UCLA, JP studied art under S. McDonald Wright. Immensely talented as an artist, he was hired by a film studio to work on the set for the film *American in Paris*.

While working on his Master's degree during summer vacations at USC with art professors D'Erdalay and Ewing, JP worked part-time for Disney Studios. Professors at UCLA and USC were magnificent teachers and helped prepare him for his future painting career.

We lived on Rivo Alto Canal in Naples, Long Beach. At the end of a summer's workday in the field of dentistry, I often found my husband excited and motivated about painting. Many times he remarked how much he wished he could paint full time.

I asked him why he didn't seriously consider doing just that. He said he felt it was impossible to make a living selling art. My response was, "Of course, it's possible! You can achieve any goal you choose and are determined to pursue."

Goals were familiar to me, while JP's life was lived one event at a time. Whatever appeared on his painter's palette, so to speak, received his attention. Some artists live as though their lives are governed by happenstance.

JP's teaching salary, combined with my even smaller income as a dental technician, didn't provide a lot of abundance. For some unexplainable reason, however, our income didn't mean to me that we were limited in what we could accomplish. Anything seemed possible.

One evening at the end of a beautiful summer day, we noticed a sign while strolling along the canal on a waterfront property. A quaint English cottage tucked under the shadow of a magnificent magnolia tree sat on the back of a corner lot. The property was for sale, and the owner's phone number was listed.

I woke the following Sunday morning with a vision of the property and the words "Buy that lot!" Turning to JP, I said, "We need to go down the canal and buy that lot." He replied, "How is that possible?" I said, "I'm not sure, but I know it is right to try."

We made an appointment with the owner of the property. The price of the lot was thirty-one thousand dollars. When the owner asked us how much we were prepared to put down, I turned to JP and asked him how much he could borrow from the Teachers' Credit Union? He replied, "Three thousand dollars." Turning back to the owner, I said, "Three thousand is the amount of our down payment." Because he felt the initial payment to be too low, the owner increased the amount of the property another two thousand dollars. With the down payment and monthly payments of four hundred dollars, we bought the property for thirty-three thousand dollars. The owner carried the paper.

Within a few weeks we moved to 143 Rivo Alto Canal. We lived there for four years with Shelley Anne, my four-year-old daughter from my first marriage. The one-room cottage had a small loft above the kitchen. JP installed a ladder for Shelley to reach her bed as well as a basket with pulleys to hoist and lower her toys and clothes.

We placed our bed behind a screen we hung from the ceiling. We had less than five hundred and fifty square feet of space, barely enough room for the three of us.

We painted the kitchen in a modern art, Piet Mondrian style. The colors were turquoise, black, red, yellow, and white. The result was vibrant. Though petite, the cottage excelled with charm.

In the late '50s, we drove north to the Monterey Peninsula as often as possible, seeking the jade-colored water, active waves, and the jagged granite rocks JP loved to paint. Over a period of time, he sketched and painted every barn and farmland from Long Beach to Mendocino, recording the subject matter permanently on canvas as a part of California history.

During each trip we went through as many of the art galleries in Carmel as possible. During the drive home, we discussed the fact that we had seen evidence of artists who painted full time. That evidence, however, didn't convince JP that he could do the same.

After considering the idea, he made an appointment with Dazzle Hatfield, owner of the Hatfield Galleries, located in the Biltmore Hotel in Los Angeles. Hatfield was widely thought of as someone who had the talent for recognizing potential in an artist's work, and JP wanted to find out if he had enough talent to leave teaching and become a full-time artist.

I arrived home from work one day just as JP was returning from the Hatfield Galleries. He got out of the car barely able to walk. I asked him what had happened, and he explained that while loading his paintings in our '59 Mercedes 190D to take to Hatfield, he fell off the curb and broke his ankle.

It was extremely painful. After helping him into the cottage so he could rest, I removed the artwork from the car.

It was amazing to me that he had driven from Long Beach to Los Angeles, removed the paintings from the car, carried them into the gallery, returned them to the car, and then drove home with a broken ankle. The fact he did showed his devotion to an idea. I was deeply impressed.

That act told me he had the necessary courage to subject his work to criticism. As far as his artwork was concerned, JP had a certain sense of his own worth. Thinking along those lines, I hurried back to the cottage to help him.

We had previously borrowed a copy of *Science and Health with Key to the Scriptures* by Mary Baker Eddy. I opened it and began to read to him at random. For the next two or three hours, JP rested and listened while I read.

When JP was more relaxed, he shared the results of his appointment with Hatfield. Hatfield told him to go home, quit his job, paint for six months and then come back with his artwork. That was very good news. It verified everything I had been feeling about the quality and the potential of his work.

We had a close friend living next door who happened to be an M.D. He stopped by to look at his ankle. The doctor acknowledged that it was broken. JP opted not to have it set, and within a few days, it was obvious that a healing was taking place. Within a few weeks, his ankle was completely normal. That was the first time we experienced healing by simply perusing the Christian Science textbook.

While living in Naples from '57 to '64, we belonged to the Alamitos Bay Yacht Club and raced small sailboats. JP was the skipper, and I was his crew. We often sailed beyond the jetty and into the choppier seas. Some of the races were on the bay at twilight, and they were our favorites.

Learning to crew was fascinating. My favorite part was putting up the spinnaker. Walking on the deck toward the bow, inserting a spinnaker poll through the brass ring on the jib, and then placing the other end of the pole through a hook on the mast, all had to be done at just the right time. The spinnaker was then hoisted up and sheeted in.

JP wasn't a kind skipper. He had a critical spirit and was quick to lose his temper. Sometimes he shouted so loudly he could be heard by the other sailors and crew. I wasn't a perfect crew person either, since almost everything he said I took personally—an indication of unresolved issues.

Most of the skippers' wives wouldn't have dreamed of crewing for their husbands. A few, however, were thoughtful enough to watch and care for Shelley while we raced. If I had been a wise and more thoughtful parent, I would have remained on the beach with Shelley and spent quality time with her. Sadly, I was too naïve in those days to understand devotion to, and the responsibility of, parenting.

I thought I was doing a much better job in that role than my mother had, but in retrospect I've seen that I could have done so much more. I only knew what I had experienced. I knew nothing about imparting a sense of love and comfort to my daughter, and that was the real problem. I simply did not understand all that a parent should be expressing to *nurture the soul* of a child.

Good parenting is something one learns through example, education, or experience. Common sense is a crucial tool, but as parents we don't always seem to use it. Wisdom was something I needed. Fortunately for Shelley, and for all of us, we didn't experience insurmountable problems. Shelley has always been intuitive, intelligent, and responsible even when she was small. Like her mom, she had to learn how to best care for herself at an early age. Reflecting on that fact deeply saddens my heart.

Over the years, we had more than one National One Design, which was a well-built seventeen-foot sloop, designed in the Midwest by a man named Crosby. It was a centerboard boat. JP knew something about sailing. I knew nothing about crewing. We learned to sail and work so well together, however, that we eventually won a First Place World Trophy in the National One Design Class.

The winds outside the jetty were sometimes as high as thirty-five knots. Strong winds often broke a backstay or even a mast. During one race, and while in first place, JP said, "The backstay is broken and the mast is about to crack in half. Should we save it by going in, or should we finish the race?"

We had just finished working on the mast. In our one-room cottage, we sanded and varnished it, retied the rigging, and installed the mast back in the hull later at the yacht club. After thinking about his question, I said, "Let's finish! Why give up first place?"

We had great times racing and competing. After sailing, we loved the barbeques with other families back at ABYC, which at that time was a small clubhouse close to Belmont Shore and directly on the beach. The clubhouse is much larger now and exists on the north side of the jetty right at the entrance to Alamitos Bay.

After approximately five years, we became weary of the National One Design and the constant work a wooden hull required, so we purchased a Victory—a twenty-one-foot fiberglass sloop.

During heavy winds, the keel design made the boat more stable. When we heeled, it seemed safer. The hull required a lot less work than the wooden seventeen-foot sloops we previously owned.

After approximately four years in a small space, surrounded by large abstract as well as representational canvases JP had painted during his Masters program, it seemed necessary to find a larger home so he could have a studio.

On another beautiful summer day, we came across a two-story home for sale, once again by the owner. I took the phone number down and called to make an appointment.

The house was priced at sixty-five thousand dollars. When the owner realized we were seriously interested, he asked how much we were prepared to put down. My response was that we would give him an immediate deposit of three thousand dollars. And, if he could give us another six months, we would sell our property and pay him an additional payment of ten thousand dollars. He agreed, and again we met the owner at the escrow office to fill out the mortgage papers. One month later, in '61, we moved into our two-story home at 33 Rivo Alto Canal.

In our new home, JP was able to spread out his paints, brushes, and canvases and leave his work however he wished. At one time, the second-story space must have been an outside porch. It had everything an artist needed. The studio floor was concrete. It had skylights and faced the canal. JP could look out the window at the boats, Naples' quaint bridges, and the sunsets reflected on the water.

Two or three months went by after placing a for-sale sign on the cottage property, but we still didn't have a buyer. Close to the fifth month, two women came to our door. They were interested in the property. We invited them in to discuss it. Before the fifth month ended, we had our ten-thousand-dollar deposit from the sale of the cottage, just as I somehow knew we would.

With a large studio, JP devoted more time to painting. As a part-time interest and further supplement to his income, he was often asked to paint signs for people. One such commission was to paint the name of a friend's boat on the stern. JP painted a name other than the one requested. Because the owner was Jewish, he thought it would be funny to paint "Jesus Saves" on the hull.

He cleverly covered the back of the boat before the owner arrived to see the result. When the canvas was removed, the owner received the shock of his life. Fortunately, he was a good sport and laughed right along with JP. The next day JP painted out "Jesus Saves" and painted in the name originally requested. Jim rarely missed an opportunity to play a joke on someone. He had a great sense of humor but could carry it to extremes.

Increasing his production had made it possible in May '59 to have the first one-man exhibit of his work. We contacted the Pacific Coast Club in downtown Long Beach and made arrangements for an exhibit. We had a collection of watercolor and oil paintings, totaling approximately thirty images.

During that month-long exhibit, Howard Booth, the manager of Paine Webber Jackson & Curtis brokerage firm, purchased two originals for his office.

I delivered both paintings to Booth's office to hang them. After climbing a ladder and hoisting the first painting to the picture hooks, which had been carefully placed several inches from the ceiling and about a foot apart, I heard someone behind me talking as though he knew me. When I turned around it was Ron Harrod. I had no idea he was a broker with the firm. It was such a surprise to see him.

Ron looked as handsome as always, and perhaps even more so. While talking to probably the only person on earth who could cause all my grace to disappear, I began to feel nervous. I don't remember what was said between us. I just know I became increasingly self-conscious.

When the paintings were hung, Ron followed me outside. The sun was beating down on the pavement. There was hardly a breeze. The air seemed literally to stand still. I could barely breathe. Everything was so quiet. I was concerned Ron might be able to hear the beating of my heart and sense my discomfort.

We talked meaninglessly for a few minutes. We were both extremely uncomfortable. I asked him about his wife and children, and if he had photographs of them in his wallet that he could show me. With noticeable reluctance, he pulled the snapshots out of his wallet and let me look at them. Then something strange happened. Ron asked me if I would have lunch with him sometime. His question surprised me. I wondered why a person who disliked me would want to see me again.

My remark was quick and to the point. "Sure," I said, "If I may bring my husband." Having no idea as to why I wanted to include JP, Ron suddenly became visibly angry, and from then on his remarks were insulting.

There wasn't any way to let Ron know my reason for suggesting that JP be included. I would never have revealed my husband's jealousy. The only way to avoid JP's intense questioning was to include him. Ron had no idea why I responded the way I did. I'm sure he just felt rejected.

I could hardly wait to get away from him. Walking back to my car, I felt my heart continuing to pound. I cried uncontrollably all the way home. I was deeply upset and terribly confused.

Though I thought of him often, it was many years before I saw Ron Harrod again. It was very strange because I lived in Naples, Long Beach, and worked full time on Atlantic Avenue not far from the offices of Paine Webber Jackson & Curtis. The confusing feelings were very aggressive. So much was left unsaid between us.

Ron stopped by to see the exhibit at the Pacific Coast Club when I wasn't there. He signed the guest book and remarked favorably on JP's talent, wishing he were as capable.

After JP's first exhibit, we had a second at an Italian restaurant, Di Piazza's, in Belmont Shore. The artwork was getting attention. The paintings were selling. That's when we discussed more frequently our goal to move to Carmel.

We wanted to open an art gallery, which we agreed I would manage, while JP painted full time. It took the better part of five years, however, to get him to resign from teaching and move north.

Meanwhile I was becoming increasingly ill. My back was hurting and was so inflamed that it was extremely difficult to work. One day I came home from work sobbing. I was in excruciating pain. It wasn't just my back. Days before I experienced a problem while swimming in the canal.

During the dive in the water, I coughed and surfaced in a pool of blood. Sometime before that, every muscle in my body started aching. My entire body was in a chronic state of pain. I felt that working full-time, attending evening classes at Long Beach State, being a mother and a wife—the busy schedule in general—might have caused the problem. Every spare minute, we were also sailing and competing in races. But it wasn't our busy schedule. It was something more.

Appointments were scheduled with doctors to try to determine what was wrong. They put dye down my lungs and took X-rays. While viewing the X-rays, one doctor asked when I had tuberculosis. "I never did," was my reply. The physician then told me I not only had it in my lungs, but that it had also spread to my abdomen. My response was that it might have been around the age of twelve when mother used to yell at me at night to stop coughing, to turn over, and stop sleeping on my back.

Learning I had had TB as a child revealed the amazing fact that for the third time I had been mysteriously healed. This time however, without any involvement of a physician or hospitalization. I wondered how those healings were possible. They were deeply puzzling to me.

The doctor's diagnosis was a condition called bronchiectasis. He advised radical right lung surgery. He informed me that without surgery I might live only another ten years.

The condition didn't explain the lower back pain, however, so I made an appointment at the UCLA Medical Center for another opinion. The doctors verified the previous lung diagnosis. Their answer regarding the back pain was a recommendation of disc surgery.

Still, no one could tell me why every inch of my body ached, so I sought out a third physician. His name was Dr. Boyle. He was an internist and partner with Dr. Smart in Los Angeles. An RUHS friend, Jerry Crail Johnson, recommended Dr. Smart's office. Dr. Smart was widely known for having successfully fought against air pollution in the L.A. basin.

In one appointment, Dr. Boyle diagnosed the problem. He said, "You're hyperventilating! Valuable nutrients such as potassium are being expelled rather than assimilated, and that makes the muscles ache."

He also put dye down my lungs and took a new set of X-rays. The X-rays revealed a small residual of dye, so he could tell I'd had them before. I hadn't told him, because I wanted a fresh opinion.

The doctor's words continued to unfold to me. "You can have surgery and become a breathing cripple the rest of your life, or you can be very careful not to catch a cold as it could lead to something fatal."

Every doctor, whether it was a back or lung specialist at the very beginning of each appointment asked the same question. *Is there something in your life you're unhappy about? Is everything all right at home?* Their questions seemed very strange. I saw no connection between my personal life and illness. JP and I had problems, and there were times when I was deeply depressed, but how could that fact relate to my physical condition, I wondered. Years later, I came to the realization that the physician's questions proved to some extent that they understood the connection between the mental and the physical cause of illness.

I took Dr. Boyle's information home with me and thought about it over a long period. While considering the surgery recommended by the first specialist and discussing it one day with JP, he made the remark that if I had surgery, I would indeed be a cripple, and he didn't want to be married to one.

I thought about the painful things he said. I didn't want to go through another divorce. As soon as possible, I purchased the Bible and the Christian Science textbook, *Science and Health with Key to the Scriptures,* for the purpose of study. I reasoned, if Christian Science heals, healing will happen! If it doesn't, I can consider the surgery.

During the summer of '64, we leased our Naples home and finally moved to Carmel. It wasn't until we moved that I actually started studying Christian Science and began to change my thought about my life and body. I wore a back brace and took nine different prescribed medications, including potassium, three times a day. This continued while I studied.

A location was found for a gallery on Dolores Street just a few doors south of the Carmel Art Association. We purchased the leasing rights. The gallery had previously marketed stoneware. We made almost no changes to the interior at that time.

We brought nearly fifty paintings with us from Long Beach. At the end of the first week, we received a letter and a check in the mail from a person who admired one of the paintings the first day we officially opened. That sale was a perfect omen!

During the first month of opening, JP often came to the gallery to help. Being there was awkward for him. He talked too much and was nervous. On more than one occasion, he dropped a painting while trying to wrap it. He gave people too much information, cracked jokes, and made them feel so uncomfortable that at least two collectors reversed their decision to purchase his work.

That experience led us to renew a previous decision. It was decided that JP would stay home and paint while I ran the gallery.

The paintings were selling so rapidly, however, we became concerned about how we could keep the gallery supplied. The entire collection of fifty paintings was sold within the first three months.

The demand exceeded the supply of work so we increased the prices. It seemed logical that if the prices were raised on the basis of supply and demand, we couldn't make a mistake.

When we opened the James Peter Cost Gallery in '64, we didn't have a painting priced higher than three hundred dollars. By the end of the sixth month, the highest-priced painting was more than five times that amount.

Very early in our gallery experience, a tall, large man came in. He showed a great deal of interest in the work. He was attracted to two small landscapes that hung over the desk by the entry.

He purchased two landscape paintings titled, "Abandoned Farm" and "Lending Neighbor." Each was an exquisite painting in egg-tempera—opaque watercolor. When he gave me the shipping address, I realized he was B.F. Dillingham of Dillingham Construction—an international company. The paintings were shipped to Honolulu.

It became increasingly common to have well-known people visit the gallery. As a resident of Pebble Beach, Leonard Firestone came in several times to purchase paintings. Ansel Adams dropped by. Walter Pigeon, Dan Rowan, Alan Funt, Lloyd Bridges, and Andy Williams stopped in eventually, as well.

From the age of seven, Shelley showed considerable artistic talent. She made hand-strung necklaces out of dyed, colorful beads. She had an extraordinary sense of color and displayed her necklaces from the age of seven in Veltman's Gallery in Naples, until we moved from there. Because of that, we were led to exhibit and sell her jewelry in our Carmel gallery.

By age eleven, Shelley showed another creative interest. She wanted to learn how to paint. Again she expressed an unusual ability to use color, but this time on canvas and in oil. She needed help with drawing, perspective, and composition, and had JP as a built-in teacher. She also benefited from her mom's marketing, sales ability, and advertising support. Her paintings started selling before she was twelve. Another remarkable quality Shelley expressed from an early age was a sense of discipline. All during her high school years, she painted. She continued painting during her undergraduate years at UCLA, where she majored in art. From the sale of her artwork, Shelley paid for her college tuition, housing, and met most of her own financial needs.

In spite of the fact that Shelley had to primarily raise herself, she has grown into a wonderful person. Most of her life, I wasn't emotionally present for her. Whether I was physically there or not wasn't the issue. Though present, I was often preoccupied with the past. Shelley survived my shortcomings and grew up beautifully in spite of them, but not without yielding to a lot of spiritual growth. She is a perfect example of devotion to a right idea.

Marriage to her stepdad was difficult. It rarely offered the affection and emotional support needed to find the peace I was searching for. I loved him and tried every way possible to show the depth of my devotion. His needs always came before mine, and that was obviously part of the problem.

I acted as if my own needs came last on the priority list; poor self-esteem was thoroughly engrained in my behavior. It was impossible for me during that time to know my own needs and wants let alone have boundaries and priorities in order.

It takes two to create an unhealthy relationship. I certainly contributed to the problem. Being closed and still in denial, it was impossible to share my true self with anyone. How could I when that selfhood wasn't known? Getting to know myself seemed like an impossible, confusing task. I considered exploring that issue by telling JP what had happened during my childhood.

After sharing the complete story, he offered no remark, not even a word. He said nothing. His lack of comfort and response was extremely painful.

At that point in my life, I needed to feel more than ever the love and comfort I longed for. His indifference made me very sad. He never discussed the issues with me. I couldn't understand his lack of concern, lack of compassion, and reluctance to express the support and reassurance I needed. It was at that point that the door to openness shut again. His cold, heartless response reinforced feelings of shame. At the time, I wondered if he felt it was somehow my fault.

Even at that stage of my growth, however, I was beginning to get the understanding that my parents were the ones who should feel miserable, not me. I was the innocent child. So, the challenge was to learn how to free myself from dwelling on past events.

Though he was handsome, very bright, and had many talents and qualities of character that were really attractive, James Peter Cost was an extremely complicated person. He wasn't at all demonstrative, and yet he was extremely jealous. He drilled me many times as to where I had been and whom I had seen.

His behavior seemed very strange in that regard because when I wasn't home, or in evening classes at Long Beach State, or later at the Monterey Peninsula College, I could only be found at work. Later in our relationship I had reasons to believe that he was suspicious of me, because he may have been untrustworthy himself.

While trying to find sanity and peace in our marriage, I ran across something interesting in *Prose Works* by Mary Baker Eddy. She was once asked what she thought of marriage. She replied: *"It is often convenient, sometimes pleasant, and occasionally a love affair. Marriage is susceptible of many definitions. It sometimes presents the most wretched condition of human existence. To be normal, it must be a union of the affections that tends to lift mortals higher."*

Our marriage seemed lovely in the beginning. Perhaps because of a lack of "union of the affections," it became only "sometimes pleasant." It broke my heart, because I very much wanted our marriage to be a solid one—happy and fulfilling for each of us.

We all loved JP very much. I believe to this day he just didn't know how to express love. He possibly thought families were about control, and the male figure was the person to fill that position. For the most part, he simply mirrored the example set by his own narcissistic father.

Though I was making huge strides toward feeling physically well, there were emotional scars that also needed healing.

People who have *not* been raised in a violent home—I wish that were everyone—have no idea why some people put up with any type of abuse.

My problem was that I thought there was only one kind of abuse—physical. I had absolutely no understanding of mental or verbal abuse. There were many deeply embedded fears that caused me to put up with abuse, but I'll share just one.

When I was quite small, my stepdad called all three of us into the Curtis Avenue kitchen. His son from a previous marriage, Robert Root, was living with us, so he was there as well.

Once we were all standing around waiting to hear why we were called there, my stepdad began beating my mother. He threw her from one end of the kitchen to the other. He didn't stop until her head was split open from the back of her skull to the front hairline and blood had splattered all over the walls.

We stood there terrified, crying and screaming for him to stop hurting our mother. To this day, I have no idea as to the reason he felt justified in beating her. Perhaps there was something he wanted her to do that she had refused. Or, and just maybe, he caught her cheating on him when he hadn't authorized it.

There was absolutely no justice in it, of course. I do know, however, that part of his reason was to instill fear in us as a means of keeping us under his control. He achieved his goal. His actions paralyzed us!

His specific demonstration of malicious hate and cruelty is just one example of what predators will do to terrorize their victims in an effort to keep them under their power. His actions showed us that, no matter what, we were not to cross Charles Earl Root! Whatever he told us to do, we did. We were all scared to death. To each of us, his height of six feet four accentuated his power.

Because of my so-called history, my life was set up for victimization. I was totally unable to stand up for myself. Until I understood how much good I deserved, how to love and respect myself, I continued to experience verbal and occasional physical abuse.

Continuing on a spiritual path and disciplining my thought through prayer began to bring occasional feelings of peace. I worked very hard to learn the art of loving myself as well as the art of true forgiveness. As I learned to refuse to accept fear as my own thought, I was eventually able to disengage from the internal dialogue caused by an abusive past. The dialogue was always present, however, until a firm, consistent effort was made through prayer to make a conscious distinction between the thoughts I wanted to accept and those I needed to reject. Until then, fear was thought's leading protagonist.

Life became a process of constantly asking questions like: Are you going to keep reliving the pain through rehearsal? Or, are you going to win the battle and find peace and dominion in spite of the past?

I learned to face, examine, and value my feelings. They gave specific clues as to what I needed to address in thought. I learned to make a conscious distinction between the thoughts I wanted to own and those that needed to be discarded. Facing each mental foe, I became stronger. Carefully choosing my thoughts, I could claim with authority, that is not my thought! That is not who I am, nor who I want to be!

Looking back over the past in an effort to forgive and let go brought progress. Clinging to the past would have prevented me from moving beyond it. Self-pity would have kept me from experiencing the healing I deserved.

Strides were made when I learned to ask for what I needed. I found the more I demanded fair treatment, the more others began to treat me with respect.

Spiritual growth is a remarkable thing. No matter where I was, or what I was doing, I always had the time to stop and think. I thought a lot about what I had been accepting as my own thought and how that determined the outcome and the harmony of my experience.

After four months of living in a two-bedroom home on Guadalupe Avenue in the heart of Carmel, JP wanted to live on the ocean so he could study the movement of the water. I called a Christian Science practitioner, as I often did when a problem needed solving, to help us find the right location. It wasn't two days before Rose, a realtor from Big Sur, walked in the gallery and asked if I was looking for a home on the water.

We leased the first house Rose showed us. It was a rhomboid-shaped home at Yankee Point, six miles south of the village of Carmel. The house was pointed in the front and pointed in the rear. It was on the ocean at the north end of Yankee Point. It was a very peculiar house, full of insects and mice, and poorly maintained by the owners. After a thorough cleaning, it met our need.

Ansel Adams was a neighbor. JP felt surrounded by creative artists. He could now paint from the living room while studying the movement of the water.

Meanwhile, I managed the gallery every day and continued on a path of praying for and expecting healing. I was still taking the medication, however, and wearing the back brace when a new friend mentioned a Christian Science lecture on healing.

The lecturer, Herbert Rieke, spoke on the oneness of God and man. While he was discussing man as the image and likeness of God, he said, "Man is the reflection of God, inseparable from Him—the very manifestation of Him." I listened carefully. I remember thinking: If man is the reflection of God, then man is as perfect as God is perfect. If God is love, and disease is not of His creating but one of finite belief, then a change of thought will make a difference.

I further reasoned: if God doesn't have a back problem, then how can I, if I am His likeness, His mirrored reflection? Continuing, I thought, If God doesn't have pain in any aspect of His being, then how can I?

While focusing intently on the message, I reasoned right along with the lecturer: if God is Love and didn't create pain, then it hasn't really happened, and it's only my belief about it and the false education I've accepted as to what constitutes my life and body, that seems to manifest pain.

Before the end of an hour, I felt a change in the condition of my back. I knew I was healed! I gained a whole new perspective on who I am and what constitutes my identity as the manifestation of God.

When I arrived home, I took off the brace and disposed of all the medication. From that day forward, I never took another pill, not even an aspirin. I no longer needed to depend on it and understood why. A poem by Samuel Longfellow summed up my feelings: "The freer step, the fuller breath, The wide horizon's grander view; The sense of Life that knows no death—The Life that maketh all things new."

The next day when Shelley was ready to leave for school, she hugged me and discovered that I wasn't wearing the brace. That's when I shared what had happened and what I'd learned at the lecture.

Shelley was thrilled. She had been attending Sunday school while I attended church. It was already making a huge difference in both our lives. We were learning something incredibly profound. Though JP didn't go along or attend, he was supportive.

Meanwhile, one of the first paintings he finished at Yankee Point was a thirty-six-by-twenty-four-inch, vertical canvas titled "Nocturne." It was a moonlight painting and breathtaking. A young man in the armed forces purchased it.

While preparing "Nocturne" for shipping and writing the inventory number, title, medium, etc., on the back of it, I was shocked to see that all the writing showed through the front of the canvas. I was terrified to think I had ruined a beautiful piece of work! I was afraid to tell my husband. Full of fear, I called a practitioner, asked for prayerful support, and explained what had taken place. He reassured me that there was a logical answer and that he would pray for me and for the situation I faced. He asked me not to mention the matter to JP right away.

The fear was almost too much to handle. I knew what had taken place was out of devotion and was not malicious. Every painting sold prior to "Nocturne" had the information recorded in the same manner. A few days later as I was leaving for work, JP followed me to the car and said the most amazing thing. He asked if I had shipped "Nocturne." I answered, "No." "Good!" he said. "Bring it home. I want to repaint the sky."

I looked at him and started crying. I was immensely relieved. He asked me what the crying was all about, so I told him what had happened. He just laughed. If the problem had been handled any other way, the result may have been very different.

We moved in '66 to the south end of Yankee Point. We purchased a home right on the ocean at Mal Paso Creek. By then we were in a better position to buy our first Monterey Peninsula home. We still owned our home in Naples, Long Beach, so we offered a reasonable deposit and immediately listed our Southern California property for sale. It sold within a short time.

Shortly after the move to the south end of Yankee Point, JP took Shelley with him on a hike up Mal Paso Creek to do some painting. That evening I heard Shelley crying in her room. I went to her to find out what was wrong. She was covered with poison oak from her lower back down to her knees. Liquid was rushing out of her skin, and the sight was terrifying.

Shelley was in a great deal of pain. I asked her if she wanted me to get in touch with a doctor, but she requested I call a practitioner. It was around eleven p.m. I hesitated to call someone at that hour, so I asked Shelley if she thought we might pray about her condition together. I didn't realize I could have called a practitioner in Hawaii as their time was two hours earlier. She agreed to our working together, so the first thing I did was to look up the word "poison" in the dictionary. The one definition that stood out to me was: "To change the character thereof." The minute I saw that definition, I knew it was the answer.

I went back to Shelley's room and told her I thought that the definition I found in the dictionary was the key. She asked what I meant. I reminded her of the fact that nothing could change her true identity or alter her God-given character. "You were created according to Genesis I in God's image, in Her likeness. You are inseparable from your Father-Mother, God. Nothing can poison or change that fact and no perfection can be taken from it. Your identity was created spiritually and not materially. The spiritual is the real. The material is the unreal. God is Love, and God created nothing to oppose His/Her law, divine Principle, to harm you. Nothing can change the spiritual fact of your being!"

We spoke along those lines for about twenty minutes, and I went to bed. In the morning, Shelley spoke with a practitioner before coming into my bedroom dressed in jeans. Thinking the jeans would bother her skin, I said, "What are you doing with jeans on?" She said, "Mom, I'm healed!" I've recalled the joy of that moment many times.

When we moved to Carmel, we still had our membership with the Los Angeles County Museum. In the spring of '66, we received one of the museum's travel brochures outlining a tour of the Orient. We decided to go, and we took Shelley with us.

We visited Hong Kong, Taiwan, Malaysia, the Philippines, Japan, and Thailand. Japan was by far our favorite country. Our trip together celebrated the new life we had chosen, which had all the signs of a very positive future.

Nancy's Here!

Family Unity

Right after the Christmas season on a Sunday morning while praying and sitting in a pew near the front of the church, I thanked God for the harmony and peace our family experienced during the holidays. Suddenly, I felt something heavy in my arms. Looking down, I saw them cradled as though they were holding an infant. I actually felt a child's heaviness. My mouth fell open. I looked up at the ceiling and quietly said, "You're kidding!" That's how I learned I was expecting my second child.

JP and I had been married eleven years. He was previously married to Harriet Bowker. They had a daughter, Janet Perry Cost, in 1950, and a son, Curtis Wilson Cost, in '53. Jan came to live with us during her last year of high school.

Jan and Shelley both attended Carmel High School. Having my stepdaughter with us was a wonderful experience. Jan was a very gentle and loving teenager.

Shelley, fifteen, and Jan, eighteen, shared the guest room, got along, and worked well together. They each had their household chores and were thoughtful about doing whatever they were asked.

To earn an allowance, most evenings after dinner, the two of them did the dishes. On the weekends, they took care of the room they shared and washed the cars. Though they must have experienced uncomfortable moments, I can't recall a single problem between Shelley and Jan. They were remarkable friends and an absolute pleasure.

On Sundays both girls went to church with me. Like most teens, they were not always happy having to get out of bed on a Sunday morning, especially after having activities the evening before. For the most part, however, their attitudes were great.

They had some outstanding spiritual teaching by some exceptional thinkers. I've often recalled the good times we shared together after the services going out to breakfast. We sometimes visited the Tuck Box on Dolores Street. The gentleman who owned it in the '60s and '70s had a gracious manner. His was probably the most service-minded restaurant in Carmel.

One serious problem we had while Jan lived with us was that JP would discipline my daughter, Shelley, while rarely, if at all, his own. One day, for instance, during the late '60s, both girls came home from high school wearing miniskirts. JP thought the skirts were far too short. He bawled Shelley out, but never said a word to Jan. I let him know he was being unfair and that I was absolutely opposed to his turning a blind eye to one daughter while scolding another. I also reminded him that it was the teenage style and told him I thought both girls handled the length tastefully. Unfortunately, it didn't prevent him from committing the same offense again.

As Shelley's parent, discipline was my priority and responsibility. A stepparent shouldn't have disciplinary control over a stepchild. Unfortunately for Shelley, I didn't have that understanding while she was growing up.

I felt more qualified to be a parent at age thirty-seven when Nancy was born. It took a long time to learn that when we love, appreciate, and care for ourselves—our own emotional, intellectual, and spiritual wellness—then we are more qualified to be a parent. It's when we have that sense of things, we are most able to help our children build self-esteem through learning to respect, love, and value themselves.

It is my belief that parenting is best done by those who are keenly aware of the immense responsibility and importance of the position. There's no greater responsibility in the entire human experience than that of being a parent!

As parents, we are literally molding human lives. The example we set is mirrored in the thinking and actions of our offspring, and the most precious gift we can give our children is to have a sound and happy marital relationship.

If, like many parents, I had waited until I was totally prepared to have children, it could have been too late. Perhaps part of the purpose in becoming a parent is the opportunity it gives us to grow with our children. Parenting teaches us so much about love.

All during the pregnancy, I continued to manage and work at the gallery. I was approximately six months along when one day I experienced a severe problem. As I was leaving the gallery for a break, I started having unusual sensations and suddenly felt wet down to my knees. I rushed to the restroom and was shocked to discover I was having a miscarriage.

Filled with fear, I closed the gallery for the day, drove home and put in an emergency call to my Christian Science practitioner. He listened carefully to the details. Then he asked me a question. He said, "How long do you intend to carry this child?" Without hesitating, my reply was, "Full term!" He gave me a specific prayerful treatment to handle the fear. After he shared some spiritual truths for me to work with, we hung up.

When I relaxed on the bed, I recalled the mesmeric suggestion that had come to me days earlier. It occurred to my thought through suggestion that I might not have to carry my child nine months. I failed to handle the thought as false and not of my own thinking. I failed to claim that God's law, and not finite belief, was governing the prenatal care and the birth of my child.

The thought to reject was the belief and fear of premature delivery—because, of course, I had every intention of a full-term delivery. I was deeply committed to doing whatever was necessary to make sure that my child had a healthy beginning. The experience taught me how important it is to be alert.

I rested for a while and soon felt well and confident enough to get up and fix dinner for my family. I was back at work the very next day. There was never another sign or threat of miscarriage during the rest of the pregnancy.

The first home we owned in Carmel was at the south end of Yankee Point. It had a private cove, Mal Paso Creek, and was right on the ocean.

On the east side of Highway One, Clint Eastwood owned 250 acres. The name of his film company, Mal Paso, came from the name of the cove.

Our Yankee Point home faced due west. The hot afternoon sun was stifling. As soon as we moved in, I started thinking about how we might change the direction of the house to southwest and shift the view toward Big Sur.

It took a while to convince JP. He agreed when I suggested that a change in design would enable him to have a beautiful new studio right on the ocean.

Since the gallery was doing well and the paintings were selling as quickly as they were finished, we felt confident enough to hire a Big Sur contractor. He developed the plans exactly as we wanted them. The result was as though we literally picked up our three-bedroom home and turned it southwest. The new addition included decks cantilevered out over Mal Paso Cove, a large studio with northern light, as well as a carport. Once the remodeling was complete, it was time to work on the décor.

The interior of our home was authentic Japanese Temple architecture, so we looked for furniture that blended well with our Asian theme. The interior walls were covered in silk. The beams were washed with a sea-like, driftwood finish, and the three-by-eighteen-inch brass fittings that tied the beams together were magnificent.

We purchased our new home at 108 Yankee Point Drive in '66. Bennett Bradbury was the previous owner. Bradbury was a Disney artist as well as a talented Carmel painter. He lived there long enough to decorate it with the best of Japanese antiques.

Bradbury's master bedroom had an antique golden Buddha approximately five feet high. It was placed on a platform in front of a wall papered in gold leaf.

Except for a few minor changes, we continued the same line of décor with rosewood furniture we designed and had made in Hong Kong.

With the house finished it was time to focus thought more on the child we were expecting. The following statements from *Science and Health with Key to the Scriptures* by Mary Baker Eddy were a great source of peace: "The offspring of heavenly-minded parents inherit more intellect, better balanced minds, and sounder constitutions. . . . [The mother's] thoughts form the embryo of another mortal mind, and unconsciously mould it, either after a model odious to herself or through divine influence. . . . Mind, not matter, is the creator. Love, the divine Principle, is the Father and Mother of the universe, including man." I knew how important my thoughts and care for myself, and our unborn baby, were to having a happy, healthy child.

Suddenly time had run out. It was a beautiful fall in '68, and we were ready for our gift. One week before delivery, I had a false alarm and checked into Carmel Community Hospital.

The following week, on a Wednesday morning at six a.m., I told the girls I was returning to the hospital, but they paid little attention. I think they thought it might be another trial run, and yet I was overdue. Sure enough, by two p.m. that day we had a baby girl.

We named her Nancy Pamela. We all adored and embraced her immediately! She arrived with two inches of black hair and smelled as pure as the fall air. I was so happy to have had her by natural birth. I would loved to have shared the event with the girls and had Nancy's delivery at home, but laws allowing home deliveries were not in place at that time.

It was an absolute joy to watch the love with which her sisters welcomed her into our family. The local paper, *The Carmel Pine Cone*, published a short article on the front page titled, "Nancy's Here."

For the first month following Nancy's arrival, I stayed home from the gallery. It was such a happy and cherished blessing to be with our new baby.

After four weeks, the person helping out at the gallery had to leave, so it was necessary for me to return to work. Before I went back, I found just the right loving, gentle person to care for Nancy. We were fortunate that the gallery didn't open until ten a.m., and it was closed promptly at five p.m.

It was important to be with our newborn as much as possible. She was so precious to care for. I loved holding, rocking, and just being with her. Having a second child was an opportunity to be a more mentally present and focused parent.

Did it bother me to leave Nancy to the care of another? Of course it did. It had always bothered me to be a working mother. It was a constant guilt trip. I struggled with it continuously.

Though the success of our business was due to the sale of JP's art, he was able to spend less than full time at his easel and work as many or as few hours as he chose, and still produce the paintings we needed to show at the gallery. We had part-time help for the gallery most weekends, but I still had to be present to manage the business at least five days a week. He felt hiring someone to replace me was not an option.

Owning and managing a gallery was a wonderful opportunity for me to develop my creative skills. After managing dental offices for more than fifteen years, I learned that running a business of my own was a lot more responsibility. While I had to deal with parental guilt, I loved the challenge of business. If the gallery failed, the blame would have been mine. It was immensely successful, however, for more than twenty-five years.

It wasn't just the work that took off, but the décor was also widely appreciated. When we redesigned and redecorated the interior, we decided on warm, dark-brown walls, complemented by a warm graphite trim (in a color similar to Payne's Grey), with at least one wall off-white. With the paintings hung under halogen lights, the walls seemed to disappear.

The color of the décor presented absolutely no distractions from the paintings, whereas light-colored walls would have demanded as much attention as the artwork. The whole effect was that of stage lighting. The interior design became so popular that other galleries copied the idea. Some actually used the same wall color and trim and installed identical fabrics, wall covering, and carpeting. Most, however, made mistakes in their effort to duplicate the effect we created.

They created dark walls without understanding the use of warm tones. Their choices were cold and uninviting. They missed the idea altogether. When viewers stepped in our gallery, all their attention was focused on the paintings. The color of the décor presented no distractions to the work.

The stage-lighting effect and décor were duplicated throughout Carmel. We chose those colors in the mid-'60s, and the idea of stage lighting is still being used in galleries. It was many years later, however, before the same color preference became a chosen favorite in restaurants and private residences.

Love for my family led me to the conclusion that it was right for all three of the girls to share the same last name. I wanted to be sure Shelley felt as much a part of our family as her sisters did. She was the only one whose last name was not Cost. So, it seemed like progress for JP to consider adoption. It took some discussion, but he finally agreed that it was an appropriate step. At the age of fifteen, Shelley's adoption was completed through the Monterey courts.

Nancy Pamela's arrival brought an extended sense of family unity and harmony. That fact inspired us to regard our collectors as an extension of family. As a result, we began to entertain thoughts of additional services we could provide. Our new view led to a unique resale system.

In the late '60s, we were receiving requests from collectors to resell the painting or collection of paintings they previously purchased, so, as a result of need, we created services never before practiced in Carmel. When a collector—due to health, divorce, or the passing of a spouse—needed to resell a painting, we took it back on consignment. The work was reappraised at the level of current value. When the painting resold, the collector received the price he originally paid for the work, and the profit was evenly shared.

The service was so successful that some of JP's original artwork resold four or five times during the thirty years we owned the gallery.

It's unlawful for galleries to guarantee an increase in value. However, it is natural for the value of a master painter's work to increase. Refraining from mass production is also important to future resale value. However, that statement can be easily disputed.

Before his death, an estimated four hundred and fifty thousand Picasso art items (paintings, sculptures, etc.) had been sold to private collectors through the various fine art dealers representing his work. Picasso left another one hundred and fifty thousand signed items in his studio ready to be sold when he passed on. The fact that he completed over six hundred thousand paintings, etc., didn't matter because he had phenomenal name recognition.

The most important part of a work of art is the painter's signature. If the artist has name recognition, his paintings will be valuable, even if the quality of his work varies. Marketing is the key.

Working at the gallery was invigorating, but nothing compared to the pleasure of caring for Nancy. She was absolutely amazing. Even as an infant, she loved to laugh. No matter what demands were made on our time, it was easy to include Nancy in our activities.

By the time she was four weeks of age, we began enjoying meals together as a family at the Beach Club in Pebble Beach, or the Monterey Peninsula Country Club at the north end of the 17 Mile Drive.

I loved the way her sisters enjoyed her, and were so willing to help with her care. Both Shelley and Jan loved and appreciated their baby sister.

We read Nancy stories and nursery rhymes from the time she was just a few weeks old. At two months, she was shown every painting hung in the house. Her favorite toy was a swing we hung from a beam in the living room. She used it as early as eight months to jump and move around. She laughed with a deep voice and a great deal of passion.

When she was nine months old, we disposed of the playpen and let her crawl all over the house. It was a lot more work to care for her, but it was beneficial to her early development.

Often while her dad was painting, Nancy would crawl on the studio floor. As she grew older, she loved sitting on her father's shoulders while he painted. One time I caught a photograph of the two of them in which JP's eyes were focused on the opaque watercolor he was working on. Nancy was sitting on his shoulders and leaning on her arm, which was placed on top of her dad's head. She watched the brush strokes as he applied them to the surface of the painting. She was approximately twenty-three months.

As her mother, there was never a time, while holding Nancy or admiring her from across the room, that I didn't feel privileged to be a parent. Those feelings were extended as readily toward our two teenagers. I was so grateful and proud of each of our children. I loved them all deeply.

It wasn't long, however, before it became obvious that our new daughter brought with her a tremendous physical challenge. She was born with deformed legs and feet. The tibia of each leg was bowed, and her feet were pigeon-toed.

Fifteen years earlier, Shelley had had the same condition. She was taken to an orthopedic surgeon for casts on her legs and a Dennis Brown Split, which she wore every night until she was four. Shoes were anchored to a steel bar. They were placed on the bar in reverse of how they would normally be worn in an attempt to straighten her feet.

As a student of Christian Science, it was natural to pray for Nancy's healing, and seek support from a practitioner. In order to demonstrate her perfection as the image and likeness of God, prayer was the first priority.

I asked the family to join me in refusing to accept any condition other than that of complete harmony and symmetry for Nancy. I found this statement in the Christian Science textbook, *Science and Health:* "The Divine Being must be reflected by man—else man is not the image and likeness of the patient, tender, and true, the One 'altogether lovely;' . . ." And in *Prose Works* by Mrs. Eddy, I found: "Everything is as real as you make it, and no more so. What you see, hear, feel, is a mode of consciousness, and can have no other reality than the sense you entertain of it."

The key to healing was to see our child as God was seeing her—whole, symmetrical and altogether lovely! Among verses from the Bible, Hebrews 12:13 was helpful: "And make straight paths for your feet, lest that which is lame be turned out of the way; but let it rather be healed." After much prayerful work, and in less than three months, her feet and legs were perfectly straight.

Sometime later, after I gave a testimony of Nancy's healing at a Wednesday evening church service, one of the ladies who cared for her in the nursery came up to me and said, "I'm glad this problem is healed. I was very concerned." I thanked her for her concern and left church feeling so very grateful for all that I was learning.

Nancy Pamela was a precious addition to our family. It was amazing how much joy her presence brought to each of us. Since she appeared to assimilate so much, we communicated with her as we would an adult. At the same time, we enjoyed and treated her as the precious child she was.

JP worked very hard the first seven years we lived in Carmel. I was proud of his devotion to a work ethic. Once we moved from Yankee Point, however, his whole sense of devotion to that ethic and production changed.

Nancy Pamela Cost on James Peter Cost's shoulders in 1970

Pebble Beach

Growth and History of Progress

JP's new interest in golf found him spending considerable time at the Monterey Peninsula Country Club. It was fifteen miles north of Hai Kuan, our home at Yankee Point. The time driving back and forth, we realized, could best be spent in the studio, so we looked at homes for sale near the club.

We favored a 1926 two-story, Mediterranean home on MPCC's Shore Course, which had a view of the ocean from every room in the house, except one. It had several bedrooms plus enough space for a studio, so we made an offer. However, we lost the opportunity to purchase the property. Wendy Waldorf of the Waldorf Hotel chain bought it to make it her western residence.

Several months after the new owner finished remodeling the house, it was back on the market. The realtor called us and asked us to resubmit our offer. Though we offered less the second time, the offer went through.

We moved from 108 Yankee Point Drive, Carmel, to 3012 Cormorant Road, Pebble Beach, in May of '71. Nancy Pamela was three. Shelley was a fine art major at UCLA, and Jan was still living with us and studying painting with her dad.

Just after we moved, friends from Long Beach came to visit. While showing our guests the master bedroom on the second floor, Nancy started jumping on our king-size bed. When she came down from a high bounce, JP reached for her leg and pulled her to the bottom of the bed. Each time Nancy crawled back toward the top of the mattress and started jumping all over again.

This continued until she was totally frustrated. Placing her hands on her tiny hips and speaking directly to her dad, she said, "Do not touch the leg, knee, or thigh!" We all stood at the bottom of the bed laughing at her indignation.

Shortly after moving in, we discovered a serious pest problem. Raccoons were living in the ceiling of the library at the south end of the house, where there was no way to reach them without breaking through the walls.

We tried many things, each of which failed. Even the SPCA wasn't helpful. Exterminator authorities told us we would have to wait until the raccoons were about three months old, and at that time the mothers would leave, and their cubs would follow. The property had a thick stucco wall around it. The raccoons lived in the wall when they left the haven of the library.

Arriving home earlier than usual on a beautiful April afternoon, I parked outside the courtyard and opened the front gate only to be shocked by what I saw at the entry. In an attempt to get to the raccoons, JP apparently had used a sledgehammer to break through the stucco. The lathe, chicken wire, tar paper, and plaster were all exposed. The view of the entry from the courtyard was a complete mess! JP and I had had several discussions as to why his desire to break through the stucco was foolish and would accomplish nothing.

Approaching the house, I realized something amazing. The whole scene had cleverly been painted. It was trompe l'oeil—an attempt to fool the eye. JP loved to fool us on the first of April, and he always succeeded.

Though it was unknown to me at the time, Nancy and her dad were inside the house peeking through the breakfast room curtains eagerly waiting for my response. They enjoyed seeing the anger build and finally a smile when I realized the whole scene was JP's clever surprise. What a guy! There were times when his sense of humor was exactly what was needed.

No matter how many times we repaired the vents, each season the little bandits broke through them again. In total exasperation, we finally went to an iron works person. New vents were designed that made it impossible for the raccoons to break through, and our pest problems were eventually solved.

It was my hope that the move to our new home would bless our family. As it turned out, it was the beginning of a very sad decline.

JP wanted his mother, Rose Perry Cost, to live with us, because she was becoming forgetful. To move her into our home, the majority of her furnishings had to be sold. Leaving Rose in her own home surrounded by her treasures, while providing full time care for her, seemed to me a more sensible plan. I was sure that changing her environment could cause her further confusion.

My mother-in-law lived in the heart of Carmel in a Victorian-style home we provided for her. It was on Ocean Avenue just one block below the village.

She couldn't have lived in a more convenient location. Rose had easy access to markets and all the shopping she could want. Her home would have been a great location for anyone taking care of her as well.

Had it been right to have Rose share our home, her presence would have blessed each of us. My reasoning as to why this was not a good decision fell on deaf ears. JP simply would not have it any other way.

Sharing our home meant additional work and more time taken away from Nancy, with whom I longed to spend as much quality time as possible. Dividing my time between Nancy and my mother-in-law seemed totally unreasonable. Care for JP's mother was exhausting.

In her right mind, Rose was sweet and loving. However, she was often confused and forgetful; her condition made her angry. Just making sure she was dressed and fed required considerable time and attention. Doctors eventually diagnosed her condition as Alzheimer's disease.

Meanwhile Roses' relationship with JP became increasingly complicated. Occasionally she thought he was her deceased husband. There were times when she took out aggressions on Nancy and treated me as an intruder in my own home. These conditions were unacceptable to me. I believe they concerned JP, too, but that he lacked the desire to make a change.

Rose was with us for approximately a year and a half before we moved her to a board and care facility. Sadly, it took a separation between JP and me for that to come about.

Before progressing that far, however, I wrote to JP's two sisters and his brother and asked them to consider becoming involved in the decision-making and care of their mother.

It seemed reasonable that some of the family members outside our household should have responded with some support. There wasn't a single answer to my plea from any of them. From that time on, I seldom heard from JP's family. I didn't want to feel angry. I was just overwhelmed.

They undoubtedly subscribed to the belief that the eldest son is supposed to care for his parent. JP played golf every day and was seldom home. Though care was provided for Rose during the day while I worked at the gallery, she required special attention evenings and weekends.

What I learned from that experience was: All children should be involved in decision-making regarding care or hospitalization of their parents. It is every offspring's obligation to see that his or her parents are properly cared for. No one individual should have to bear the entire responsibility.

During this difficult time, my daughters were my source of strength and inspiration. Shelley was continuing her study at UCLA. She was doing an unbelievable job of working at her studies as well as painting for the gallery.

Not too long after our move to Pebble Beach, JP received a second commission from *Reader's Digest.* His first commissioned painting appeared on the June '69 cover and the second was on the May '72 cover.

Success stories and advertisements of JP's work placed in national magazines, such as *Art in America, Connoisseur, Southwest Art,* and other magazines, drew the attention of the R.W. Norton Museum in Shreveport, Louisiana. The museum extended JP an invitation for a one-man show. In October of '71, thirty paintings were gathered from collectors all across America and loaned to the museum. The show was extremely successful.

In '73, he finished his most famous landscape titled, "The Yellow Truck." Inspiration for the scene came from a painting trip along Highway 46, which runs east and west between Highways 5 and 101. Paul and Norma Foster of Foster Farms purchased the original, but not before we published a collotype of the painting in New York at Triton Press. We preferred this process because it eliminated the half-dot tones found in the four-color lithography process used for lithographs and posters.

In '77, we met Governor Ronald Reagan in Pebble Beach. We were deeply impressed with the results of his leadership in California. Before he was elected President in '80, we decided to express our appreciation in an unusual way. JP had just completed a beautiful transparent watercolor titled, "All the Things I Should Have Done, I Did!" We wanted Governor Reagan to have the painting. He graciously accepted our gift.

The painting was shipped to Sacramento, and, like the gentlemen he was, he called the gallery to thank us and later sent a letter to let us know how much he and Nancy enjoyed the painting.

We learned the transparent watercolor hung for several years in the dining room of the Reagan Ranch in Santa Ynez Valley. When the ranch was sold to the Young America's Foundation, we were told they received the painting. They presently have it displayed in their offices on State Street in Santa Barbara.

In the mid-'70s, we submitted a seascape of JP's to a national competitive exhibit for marine artists hosted by Franklin Mint. Over five hundred painters competed. JP won first place, a gold medal, and five thousand dollars for his entry, "Sand and Rocks at Pebble Beach."

As our gallery continued to progress, we wanted to do something in the fine art field within the community and outside of the gallery. We were members of the Beach Club in Pebble Beach. The club exists in an exquisite location near the Del Monte Lodge overlooking Stillwater Cove. We contacted the manager, and in '76 a family group showing was arranged.

By this time, Curtis' paintings were well received on Maui, so we invited JP's son, Curtis Wilson Cost, and his wife Jill, a batik artist and entrepreneur, to exhibit with JP and Shelley. We included Jan's work, since she had just completed a few paintings while studying art with her dad. Nancy had one painting in oil and one in watercolor in the exhibit. I collected the work, hung it, and did the appropriate marketing.

Clint and Maggie Eastwood attended the show. Clint's parents were neighbors of ours. We were so shy we barely knew how to acknowledge our honored guests. Memory tells me that none of us seized the moment to openly express our appreciation for their presence, but we certainly felt it.

The *Monterey County Herald* took a Cost family photograph. It appeared soon after on the front page of the art section of the paper.

We witnessed an historical event at Cormorant Road in '77 when Gerald Ford stepped down from the office of President of the United States. The President flew directly from the White House to the Monterey Peninsula to play in the AT&T golf tournament. There was so much rain that January that the Spyglass Golf Course was rained out, so the Monterey Peninsula Country Club Shore Course was the replacement.

By the time President Ford arrived to join that day's playoffs, the tournament had already begun. He was dropped off from his limo on the 17 Mile Drive in front of our home.

The President teed off on the twelfth hole and hit the ball directly up on the green. While he was putting, we called Nancy down from her bedroom to watch President Ford tee off on the thirteenth hole. She ran down stairs, barefoot with shoes in hand, and sat on the porch tying them while the President stepped up to the tee. He hit a shot straight down the center of the fairway.

Our home on Cormorant Road was the largest on the golf course, but it was very unattractive. The architectural design looked like a boring, two-story box. We spent sometime visualizing a new living room on the front of the house with the roofline wrapped around the north end.

Changing the exterior design was essential to the appearance. In the late '70s, we hired a builder who had previously remodeled two of our gallery locations. We had all the ideas worked out as to how the new living room and roofline should look. We wanted windows all across the front of the new living room to face the ocean.

Our home on the thirteenth hole of the MPCC Shore Course overlooked the ocean and the 17 Mile Drive. When the remodeling was finished, the new design had all the pizzazz it needed.

The majority of JP's works were Plein Air paintings sometimes sketched and only partially painted on location during the painting trips we took together. Several times we drove across America just for the purpose of obtaining subject matter. Our happiest times as a couple occurred during the trips we took together.

Johnny Pott, a professional golfer and collector of JP's work, won the Crosby Pro Am (later called the AT&T) in '68. Johnny designed the Carmel Valley Ranch Golf Course with Jerry Barton, who was the owner of the ranch at that time.

Jerry and Johnny commissioned JP to paint a thirty-by-thirty-six-inch painting of the thirteenth hole at CVR. The painting was finished in '81. At the time the original was delivered, Johnny didn't know there were over twenty animals painted and hidden in the trees and shrubbery. "Carmel Valley Ranch From The 13th" was on exhibit in the CVR Club House for some time before he realized the hidden surprises.

Whenever he could, JP would do something totally unexpected in his paintings, and in life itself, to express his insatiable need for humor. Fortunately Johnny Pott was a good sport and totally enjoyed the discovery.

Nancy graduated from Carmel High in '85. Her near eighteen years seemed but a few. I was deeply saddened when it came time for her to move away. She moved to Westwood in Los Angeles to attend UCLA as a design major.

During this period a small group of Japanese businessmen came to Carmel to commission an artist to paint several original paintings of golf courses in Japan. After seeing our gallery, JP's work was chosen.

He was already well-known for some of the most famous golf course scenes in Pebble Beach. The fifteenth at Cypress, Spyglass Hill, the Monterey Peninsula Country Club, the infamous seventh hole on the Pebble Beach course as well as Muirfield in Dublin, Ohio, were just a few golf course scenes JP painted.

Many of the golf originals were reproduced on covers of California magazines. Each golf scene painted was reproduced, and the collection sold out quickly.

The commission included all expenses paid for an entire month in Japan. It even included an interpreter and a driver. Since it wasn't possible for JP to manage the schedule and equipment alone, the invitation included both of us. In order to sketch all the scenes lightly in oil on canvas in one month, JP's time had to be highly organized.

The employer was a young businessman named Hirosaki. He and his associates commissioned JP to paint Meishin Yokaichi, Pine Lake, Rokko Kokusai, Oak Hills, and Seve Ballesteros Golf and Country Club.

We visited Tokyo, Osaka, Kyoto, and Takamatsu. Because we had been in Japan on a museum tour twenty years before, the return trip was even more enjoyable.

The most impressive scene was on the Meishin Yokaichi Golf Course. One day, just as the long afternoon shadows were cast across the course, approximately thirty to forty women, dressed in appropriate Japanese attire, including white aprons and coolie hats, began sweeping the green with large handmade brooms. They moved in unison down the course to the next tee. It was a visual symphony and sight exquisite enough for a painting. We watched them, mesmerized by their presence and the beauty of the sunlight framed by the long afternoon shadows.

By the end of the month, the sketching of the five courses was complete. We returned home so JP could finish the work on the originals. Each was made into a stone litho, and the well-known Japanese artist, Tsubota, was selected to assist Jim in that process.

The trip to Japan was successful except for one thing. We were invited to a private home while we were in Osaka. The businessman's mother, wife, and children were present at the meal. During dinner, the host said, "My wife, she drinks too much." I thought to myself, no wonder!

Almost every night during the month spent in Japan, we were taken to gourmet sushi restaurants. Most of the time, this same gentleman had his mistress with him. We learned that it was an accepted part of the Japanese culture to have as many mistresses as affordable.

Having seen him with his mistress, there was no confusion as to why his wife "drank so much." What a demeaning way to face marriage! Perhaps this custom is accurately defined in *Prose Works* by one of Mrs. Eddy's definitions of what marriage at its worst can be—"the most wretched condition of human existence."

Having worked part-time for the gallery, Shelley managed it while we were out of the country. It was such a relief to have the support of someone who was dependable, trustworthy, and talented with potential clients. Long before then, Shelley had become one of our most successful artists. She was naturally talented. We thought of her ability and devotion to the gallery as an added gift.

A year or more after the visit to Japan, and as a graduation gift, Nancy and I took a trip to Europe together for a month. We visited Italy, Switzerland, France, and England. We spent a week in each country. Seeing artwork and sculpture we'd read and studied about was a wonderful experience to share.

All her life, Nancy Pamela has been a caring, loving, and supportive daughter. Our trip and the time spent with her will always be among my most treasured memories.

On an afternoon when I wasn't expected home early from the gallery, I noticed the answering machine blinking. Stopping to listen to the message, I heard a young woman's voice say, "Why haven't you stopped by recently?" I knew the message wasn't a prank, because I had heard what seemed to be the same voice and similar message on the machine sometime before.

I ignored it the first time, thinking it might be someone playing a joke, or that it might be a mistake. This time, as in the first message, the woman simply started talking as though she expected JP to pick up the phone. The message came at a time when it was known that I would be at the gallery and on a day when he had an early morning appointment, so JP missed the call.

JP had mentioned her name previously several times. He went to great length to tell me about the deer she fed and how one of them was so tame she often let it in her house. After he talked about his friend for some time, I got the distinct impression that their relationship was more than friendly. Apparently, he sometimes dropped by her house while playing golf. During daylight saving time, JP often went out on the course again before dark, even if he had played golf earlier in the day.

It was sad to realize I no longer felt concerned as to how he was using his time. It wasn't even necessary to confront him. Expressing the love and support I felt for JP left me exhausted. It rarely seemed reciprocal. I had so hoped to receive from him the affection and marital unity I longed to experience.

I finally reached the point where I knew I deserved to be treated with more respect and gratitude as his wife and working partner. The marital fences could have easily been mended with the right words at the right time, sincere affection and devotion to our family unit. It never happened. What a shame. How very, very sad!

An affair never occurred to me as an option. Had it been a desire, opportunities were available.

As a wife and mother, it was important to set the right example and do the very best I could to be a good and loving parent. Being present physically, mentally, and spiritually for my family was the priority. Though I often fell short of being completely focused, I loved each of them deeply and wanted with all my heart to give my children a family life they could be proud of, an example for their own future.

From my own childhood perspective, I knew the value of a peaceful, loving home, and that was the gift I wanted for them. At the time, I believed our home was a reflection of those qualities.

As a family living in Pebble Beach, we had all the "appearances" of talent and happiness. Shelley and Nancy didn't need just pleasant appearances, however. What they needed was quality time with their parents, a safe, loving home—a place of comfort.

One parent can set a good example, but what better gift than to be a united couple. A sound, harmonious relationship in marriage is the greatest legacy parents can leave their children. A home where offspring love to return is something they will remember all their lives.

My marriage to JP lasted for thirty-two years. Just staying together, however, isn't enough of an example for one's children. They need to witness a quality relationship between their parents in order to help them develop meaningful relationships later in life. Children need a peaceful environment in order to give them the hope and faith it takes to demonstrate the same in their adult lives.

Staying together for the sake of one's children can set children up for failed relationships. If it seems to be impossible for a couple to become a "united front" and set the right example, then the best thing for everyone, especially the children, is to move on. I've heard Dr. Phil say, "It's always healthier for children to be from a broken home rather than living in one."

A discordant marriage between parents can become an opportunity for their offspring to seek guidance from a church minister, therapist, or to take advantage of a self-help process. In any case, it is an opportunity for spiritual growth.

Constant communication, spiritual unity, and working together are some of the preferred tools of marriage. A good marriage reflects regeneration and renewal. It takes a ready, ever-present sense of gratitude—remembering all the reasons you both initially felt love for and attraction to one another—to keep from falling into stagnation and selfish boredom.

We had been living in a state of emotional divorce for years. Now, however, divorce began to take on a more active plan. My need was to think about the rest of my life and what could be done to give it direction and focus.

The era of denial actually worked against my future. We owned considerable property, which over the years had been sold off piece by piece. There were two houses in Carmel on Ocean Avenue, a house south of Ocean Avenue on Camino Real, the ocean front house overlooking Mal Paso Creek at Yankee Point, a lot across from the ocean on Spyglass Golf Course and 17 Mile Drive in Pebble Beach, and finally our home on Cormorant Road with a view of the Pacific Ocean from Cypress Point to Point Joe. These were real estate acquisitions made after our move to Carmel from Naples, Long Beach, and purchased after the gallery became successful.

After living in Pebble Beach for some time, I had many discussions with JP regarding retirement. If he wanted to paint less, or not at all, and spend his time playing golf, I told him that was fine. If that was the case, it seemed reasonable and logical that we both enjoy retirement.

I tried reasoning with JP regarding the several pieces of property we purchased during our marriage. My question was always the same. Why not sell everything off, put the funds in an interest-bearing account, and live off the interest? If we had, neither of us would have had to continue working.

There was another distinct attitude occurring as well. JP wanted to keep the gallery and have me run it. However, he wanted a new marketing agent. As he saw it, the reproductions of his work, and an occasional original, could still be sold through our gallery, while the main part of his production would be handled by a new agent and represented through galleries outside of California.

The idea was a good one, but it had three major flaws. First, having only one or two originals in a gallery can't be successful unless an artist has phenomenal name recognition. It takes showing a collection of an artist's work to sell his paintings. Secondly, for the past several years, JP hadn't been as interested in painting, so how did he expect to supply a new agent with artwork? When an artist's work is shown in more than one gallery, he has to be a prolific painter in order to meet gallery demand. Lastly, his plan was not a solution for both of us.

After spending over thirty years developing JP's career, it was extremely disappointing to have collectors return to the gallery to find little or nothing available. They often came back to add to their collection.

We tried exhibiting several other artists' work. Because most viewers came to see and purchase work by James Peter Cost, selling other artwork didn't work well for the gallery, unless it was paintings by Shelley Cost or Curtis Wilson Cost.

As long as there were new images to varnish, inventory, frame, and sell, working at the gallery was extremely interesting. When we had only prints and one or two originals to exhibit, the gallery seemed more like a store and became confining to me.

After so many years spent managing and working full time at the gallery, it began to feel imprisoning. The whole activity lost interest for me. It was the creativity and financial challenges that made owning a business exciting.

JP wanted to keep all of our acquisitions, including stocks and other investments. In order to be a successful artist, he felt he needed to be able to afford our property and eliminate the appearance of having to paint for a living. I told him his was a losing plan. One can't appear to be something they are not. Either he had to continue painting or we needed to consider new alternatives to making a living.

The longer we lived at Cormorant Road, the less he painted. To supplement our income, we sold off one piece of property after another. Had perspicacity been foremost in my thought, I would have insisted on keeping one or two property investments. I still hadn't learned the wisdom of listening to or thinking about my own needs in order to care for myself.

As the gallery became less than a creative force, I eventually realized if I arranged the sale of the gallery, JP would have to agree because I was co-owner. Shortly after this realization, a gentleman came in to ask for the fourth time to purchase the lease. This time I listened. His persistence finally got my attention.

I turned away from him long enough to write down on a piece of paper the amount necessary for him to pay in order to purchase our lease. After doubling the amount, I took the paper with the new figure on it, placed it in his shirt pocket and said, "If you can meet our price, you may purchase the lease." He said, "Fine!" I replied, "Aren't you going to look at the amount?" He said, "I'll pay whatever you're asking." He did, and the escrow closed within a few weeks.

Over the twenty years we lived in Pebble Beach, it occurred to me several times to file for divorce. We separated at least twice before final action was taken.

I felt such sadness to be breaking up my children's home. Though Shelley was a full-time professional artist and a mature adult, and Nancy was in her last year at UCLA, I realized there would never be an appropriate time to leave their father and the life we built together, and yet I knew I had to move on.

A family is never the same after divorce. It can be terribly sad for the offspring. The family gatherings, as we had known them, would no longer exist. It broke my heart to take this step and to disappoint our children.

It was extremely difficult to change my life and be responsible for change in the lives of so many others. An infinite source of strength was necessary in order to move on.

When two people are unhappy with one another and their life together isn't what it should be, it is easier to stay with the ship than to test uncharted waters. To instigate change is frightening. It takes courage to change one's life. It takes moral courage to make a change. It's easier to turn around, go back, and settle for what is familiar since it seems comfortable. Feelings of familiarity can be obstacles to keep us from moving forward.

Why would divorce be an example of moral courage? When you deserve more, why would you settle for less! Why would you subject yourself or your children to an unhappy environment? Why would you settle for less than what you need or what you and your offspring rightfully deserve?

Witnessing their parents' unhappy marriage has left a lot of adults very sad. If we take that example and resolve to find the key to a higher sense of partnership, we have used adversity to an advantage.

JP had someone in his life before the divorce was finalized in '89.

Two extraordinary airport events happened to me that same year. Every summer since '66, I'd traveled to Chicago to attend a weekend seminar. On the way there in '89, the United Airlines flight I took developed hydraulic problems, so the plane had to land in Denver. Before the passengers left the plane, the pilot announced to those of us who needed to fly on to O'Hare Airport that two United Airlines flights would soon be leaving from Denver for Chicago. The first was to leave in twenty minutes and the second within an hour.

I walked rapidly toward the nearest gate, where I could board Flight #232 leaving within minutes. On my way to the gate, I saw a friendly-looking man standing in the middle of the airport stopping people and shaking hands. As I approached him, I wondered, what is his name? Because I am accustomed to doing so, I prayed, "Father, what is this man's name, for I know I know him!" The answer came immediately, "Rosie Grier."

As I moved closer, Rosie smiled, extended his arm, and offered a friendly handshake. He asked, "What are you doing with your spiritual life?" My response was one of laughter. I said, "What an unusual question to ask in a busy place like this." With that, we sat down, and I told him that I was a student of the Bible and believed in the healing that the study of the Bible afforded.

I complimented him on the results of his work with young people. We talked for several minutes, and because I had missed the first flight, I headed toward the second gate.

When I arrived in Chicago, Shelley reached me by phone at the hotel to ask if I was all right. She told me that United Flight #232 had crashed in Sioux City, Iowa, killing 110 of its 285 passengers.

Though deeply sad to hear the news, there wasn't a doubt in my mind that my encounter with Rosie Grier had prevented me from boarding the flight that crashed on July 19, 1989. And there wasn't a doubt that the protection I experienced was the result of prayer.

When it was time to leave Chicago, I heard Ron Harrod's name spoken over the speaker at the O'Hare Airport. He was being paged to pick up the white courtesy phone. The fact he remained in my thought for over forty years tempted me to page him. Though I was divorced, Ron probably was still married, I reasoned, and I wasn't about to contact a married man, so I never responded to the tempting thought to pick up the phone.

It was approximately three years after my divorce before I felt interested in companionship again. During that period, I took plenty of time for study and growth, time to grieve and heal.

I remarried in '92. Unfortunately, remarriage didn't prevent me from making another mistake. I married a person who seemed to have the right qualifications important in a partner. I couldn't have been more wrong! It was a complete disaster except for the fact that he had a wonderful young son. My new stepson and I were close during the time his father and I were married. Out of consideration for him, and because he had never really had a mother remain in his life, I waited seven years until he graduated from high school before I divorced his dad.

Through study and growth I realized I needed to heal my thought of the belief of victimization. Easily deceived, we become prey to those who would use us. If loneliness is not addressed, it can set us up for wrong relationships. Acknowledging that fact can open our eyes to what may otherwise be a totally inappropriate relationship.

The first step is to gain a right sense of who we are and how very much good we deserve. Examining our thinking, we can be healed of attracting the wrong type of person.

It was another three years or more before I was ready to consider companionship again. With my record, I probably should have made a commitment to be single the rest of my life. But my heart had a huge ache, which hadn't been filled since I was a young woman of sixteen.

From left to right: Janet Perry Cost, Shelley Anne Cost, James Peter Cost, Nancy Pamela Cost, age 8, BettyJo Cost, Curtis Wilson Cost, and Jill Cost, in a 1976 *Monterey County Herald's* photograph

Marriage
is
sometimes
a
Love Affair

Reconnecting

Answer to Prayer

Five months after Ron Harrod's wife passed on, he was ready to move on with his life. A neighbor of his found Ron's name in the RUHS Alumni Directory and loaned him her copy. Up to that point, neither had known the other attended the same high school. My address was listed in the directory as Maui, Hawaii.

Ron asked his eldest daughter, Janeanne, to try to locate me during one of her frequent business trips to Hawaii, and she agreed.

I went to Maui in 1999 to finish coordinating the remodeling and refurbishing of a second Curtis Wilson Cost Gallery, opening on Front Street in Lahaina. His first gallery opened in '84 in Upcountry at the Kula Lodge. Before I left for Maui, I had attended a 50th reunion in Southern California of the RUHS Class of '49.

At the reunion, I saw many classmates. One of them was Dewey Falcone. Another was Rosalie Fritzen Esser. It was wonderful being with and seeing familiar faces of what had seemed like lost friends.

I also saw a former neighbor, Doreen Murphy, with whom I had a very short and extremely uncomfortable conversation. She knew my parents, so I made the remark that they were awful people. Doreen jumped all over me. "They weren't awful!" she said. "I knew your parents. They were kind and generous." I looked at her in total disbelief. I was totally shocked by what she said. Obviously she thought I was out of my mind for having referred to them as awful.

I wondered how she thought she knew them. How can anyone really know a person unless they've lived with that person? And it was her good fortune that she didn't! Doreen reminded me of my mother, E.T., who lived by a unique system of denial. If she hadn't witnessed an event, she was convinced it didn't happen.

I was deeply bothered by Doreen's remarks. Had her friendship been genuine, I believe she would have listened to what was said and felt empathy for a situation she obviously never really understood.

Leaving the reunion, I was filled with emotion. While I was happy to see familiar faces, I was troubled by old feelings, because of Doreen's attitude. It wasn't long, however, before I began to forgive her remarks. After all, there was no way she could have known the truth. Nothing was ever mentioned to anyone inside or outside of our home while I was growing up.

As I left the reunion, I signed the alumni book and listed my new address on Maui.

When I arrived at the Maui airport, Curtis' mother, Harriet Bowker Cost, was waiting to pick me up. She graciously asked me to be her guest in her Wailia home until I could find living accommodations of my own. I lived with Curtis' mother for two months before moving to Lahaina Shores on Front Street.

Living on the island was a huge adjustment for me. Full-time residents have no idea as to the challenge it can be for mainlanders to live and work there. The open spaces and highways on the mainland provide such a sense of freedom as opposed to the restrictions of an island. From one end of Maui to the other, there is only one two-lane highway. In retrospect, I can say I am not a full-time island person; however, I thoroughly understand why people love Maui. It has all the beauty and peace most are seeking. And my stepson, Curtis, knows just how to capture that beauty on canvas.

Working with Curtis and his wife, Jill, who is also his business partner, was a very good experience. I love the fact that his galleries are run by the two of them. They have mirrored the same sense of principle and devotion to an idea as demonstrated previously on the mainland in our gallery, the James Peter Cost Gallery. They feature the best in quality and offer a similar sense of service.

Curtis and Jill showed me the most loving sense of concern and caring by offering me a position in their new location. It came at a time when I needed something positive in my life.

I worked as the director of their Front Street gallery in Lahaina. While I was there, the value of Curtis' original paintings more than doubled. The new gallery was successful and well received from the very beginning. Like his father's artwork, the demand far exceeded the supply.

It was two years before I returned home to Carmel. I couldn't wait. In all that time I hadn't seen my close friends and rarely my daughters. I missed them terribly. I was home approximately fourteen months before I received an e-mail from the Maui gallery saying that Ron Harrod was trying to reach me.

Ron and BettyJo in 1947

A Change of
Consciousness

Brings the Goodness Desired

Spring brought with it the desire to have companionship again. After three marriages ending in divorce, I was naturally hesitant.

One night when I was feeling depressed, I realized that prayer was needed. A long-time friend had asked me to join him for dinner and a movie. I liked him, and we had much in common; however, I felt reluctant.

Sitting in a comfortable wingback chair, I prayed. Christian Science taught me that scientific prayer amounts to reason, revelation, and demonstration and that a change of consciousness brings the goodness desired. I reasoned, "Father, I have outlined my relationships all my life. The first time I married, I wanted a home, the second time a husband and father for my daughter, and the third time I thought the best relationship I could possibly have would be with a church member. Surely a church member would be genuinely faithful and responsible."

"None of those reasons were totally right. I really don't feel comfortable, Father, in accepting this or any other invitation until You give me some indication that being with someone, whether now or in the future, is what You want for me." I also said, "I can't do this any more. I can't go on outlining my life. I'm going to sit here until You tell me who I'm to see or what offer of companionship I am to accept. My life is in Your hands, Father. I can do nothing of myself, but You can do all things! It is Your will I am seeking."

Feeling satisfied that the direction of my life was placed directly in God's hands and governed by Him, I got up out of the chair and went to bed.

The next day I continued praying and began to feel more at peace. I let go of the whole idea of seeing or being with someone any time in the future. I felt free. My thought was no longer preoccupied or burdened by feelings of loneliness.

One morning, several days later before going to work, I checked the Internet to see if I had mail. My stepson, Curtis, had sent an e-mail from Maui informing me that Ron Harrod was trying to reach me. It listed his phone number and e-mail address. I couldn't believe how excited I felt! Just seeing his name caused my heart to beat as rapidly as it had more than fifty years ago.

I sent an e-mail to Ron right away. I asked him where he was living and told him that I was under the impression he was out of state, perhaps in Chicago. I explained that in July '89 on one of my trips to Illinois, I heard his name announced at O'Hare Airport requesting he pick up the white courtesy telephone. I told him I was tempted to have him paged. He verified the fact that he was at O'Hare in July that same year.

When I arrived at work and couldn't keep my mind on the job at hand, I called Ron. He told me he had been living in Southern California all his adult life.

Ron had been married for more than fifty years and had two daughters, Janeanne Harrod Rinaldi and Kitty Harrod Smith. His wife, Jodeane Collins Harrod, had just passed on that previous October. He talked about her a lot and seemed quite depressed. As he spoke, I listened intently and could feel his sadness. I smiled, however, at being able to speak to him again.

For two weeks we talked several times each day and sent e-mails and faxed back and forth. We caught up on what had been happening in one another's lives. We discussed how we broke up in the '40s and how we spoke briefly each time we accidentally ran into one another.

I received this apology from him by e-mail: "Our friendship never ended as for me. My mother insisted it was unfair of me to demand a relationship with you when I was away at school most of the time. She convinced me. She was a very good sales person. I regret my rudeness to this day and have spent years recriminating and mulling over my nasty, unnecessary tactics. You were one of the nicest people in the world and did not deserve such shabby treatment. This is one reason I got in touch with you. Before I leave this earthly place I need to apologize and acknowledge my stupidity. I have not liked myself over these wrongs. You have been foremost in my mind for fifty-plus years. Your picture, you know, has been in my desk all these years. I hope I may be understood and forgiven."

At the time, if I had known the reasons he dumped me, I wouldn't have understood his mother's reasoning. Fifty-six years later, it made a lot of sense.

The more I thought about his letter, the line, "This is one reason I got in touch with you," echoed in my head all day. What are the other reasons, I wondered? Why else did he contact me? The fact that he kept four pictures of us all those years and had looked at them occasionally was remarkable.

I couldn't stand it any longer. I had to see him. I called and asked what he was doing for Easter. He said he had no plans.

I asked for an additional day off from Classic Art Galleries. I'd worked there as an art consultant since returning to Carmel from Maui. On Easter weekend, I drove to Newport Beach to visit Ron.

It was nearly noon when I arrived at his home. I was so nervous I could barely think. He lived in a beautiful neighborhood. It was quiet and well manicured. I pulled up to the garage, checked out my makeup in the rearview mirror, and tried to walk slowly down the long entryway to his front door. I pressed the doorbell. It was a very long minute before he answered. When Ron opened the door, he invited me in and we hugged for what seemed like a very long time.

At the end of the embrace, he walked very rapidly toward the north end of the living room and sat down behind an oversized partner's desk. I stood on the other side of the desk and looked around for a chair. There was a rocking chair a few yards away, but there wasn't a chair close by.

Laughing while still standing, I asked, "So where am I to sit?" He kept right on talking, so I repeated the question, "Where should I sit down?" Still amused at the fact that he was hiding behind a desk—for it was a barrier between us and obvious to me that he was nervous—I beckoned him to the eight-foot couch where we sat down and talked. While we were both still standing, however, we embraced and kissed for the first time in fifty-six years.

When we sat down, the feelings were extremely strange. It was though we had never been separated. We communicated easily and had such empathy for one another. We both felt as though we were still in our teens, no time had passed, that it was still '47 and we were in his '46 Mercury. Instead of saying good-bye, we were unwilling to let go. We sat there on the couch talking and looking at one another for a long while.

Having just finished a five-hour drive from Carmel, I suddenly felt tired. Rising by three a.m. to leave Carmel by five, I asked if I might stretch out in the guest room for twenty minutes or so. It was impossible to rest, however, knowing he was in the next room. I went back in the living room, pulled him out from behind the desk again, and led him back to the couch where we continued talking.

We talked for hours. We finally had the conversation we should have had when we were young. We discussed what had happened in our lives while still in our teens.

I learned a lot about his relationship with his wife, their family, and his work. Ron stayed with the brokerage firm, Paine Webber Jackson & Curtis in Long Beach, for a long time. When the company went public, it became an entirely new organization where standards changed dramatically.

After eleven years, Ron left Paine Webber Jackson & Curtis. He witnessed transactions that were totally out of line with his sense of integrity, perception of service, and protection of the client.

The next brokerage Ron joined was Dean Witter and that was a great company as long as Witter was alive and managing it. When he passed on, the company developed the same inconsistencies.

Brokers bought and sold stocks assigned to them just for the sake of earning commissions. They seemed to have little or no regard for how an acquisition might produce benefits or losses for their clients.

At that point, Ron became an independent investment advisor. As an independent, he could invest his client's money in what he would choose to invest his own savings in. He was free from brokerage firms insisting he sell something they needed to move off the shelf. Ron just wanted brokers to do right by their clients.

On Easter Sunday, we went to the Pelican Club in Newport Coast. My daughter Nancy joined us for an Easter brunch.

The weekend ended with the full realization that I was very much in love with Ron. That fact had never changed. There was absolutely no question about it. Nothing changed those original feelings during the more than fifty years of separation.

Back in Carmel and unable to sleep one evening, I got out of bed and went to the computer. I was really worried about Ron. He didn't have the confidence and pride of the young man I once knew. He had low self-esteem and acted as though he felt he had failed—failed himself, his wife, and in the business community. He was very ill. His face and his whole body was that of a very sick man. During the time spent with him, I could literally feel Ron clinging to life.

Deeply concerned and worried, I e-mailed him the following: "It's a little after 3 a.m. I'll try to put down some thoughts, which have been attempting to express themselves for sometime: Your wife promised to make you happy. And, I know you were. You had a good life together, a beautiful family, status in the community, many friends and much more.

"However, I'm not convinced that you achieved happiness. It isn't something one can give us. It's a gift we give ourselves. Like Jodeane, I am promising you happiness. However, my devotion will not be to GIVE you happiness and contentment. My devotion to you will be to make sure that YOU GIVE yourself happiness—a thorough appreciation and love of your own identity, as well as: An absolute redemption of criticism of self; recognition of your own potential and worth; regeneration of thought—thoughts of wellness and wholeness; a loosening of false concepts of health; freedom from a false sense of responsibility; an acceptance of yourself as God's child—whole and complete! You have one important, magnificent person to care for, and that is yourself!

"Yes, I want to be there to make sure you do all these things. I don't want to be with you to MAKE you happy! I want to be with you to make sure YOU bring the happiness you deserve to yourself.

"Loving you is one of the three greatest gifts I've ever received. And I know that until I learned to value and love myself I wasn't the whole person you deserve."

It was about four a.m. when I finished sending the e-mail. Ron was so much in my thought that I was led to embrace him in prayer, knowing God's love for him was filling his thought and heart with all that he needed to feel healthy, successful and happy once again.

My understanding of true happiness is appropriately expressed in Oprah's book, *What I Know For Sure*: "The happiness you feel is in direct proportion to the love you are able to give."

Thy Faith Had Made Thee Whole!

One Source of Intelligence

Every day while working in Carmel for Classic Art Galleries, I expected Ron to walk in the door. He never did. Sometime later I realized it was impossible for him to make the six-to-seven-hour drive it could take to travel north from Newport Beach to Carmel.

Ron couldn't sit very long. He was in a great deal more pain than he was admitting. So, his choice of transportation on Mother's Day was to fly, but even that was excruciatingly painful. It wasn't just sitting and waiting for the flight or flying; it was the extensive walking he had to do between airport terminals. When I arrived the airport to pick Ron up, he looked very ill.

We collected his bags and headed to my apartment. We had a chance to talk for a while before my family began to arrive for the day's celebration.

It still wasn't clear as to what was going on with Ron, so I began questioning him more carefully regarding what he was struggling with. He was reluctant to talk much about his condition. He admitted, however, he hadn't seen a doctor in many years.

During our conversation, Ron excused himself to go to the bathroom. When I went in later, I discovered the key to his problem. He hadn't flushed the commode and it was full of blood.

I immediately went to him and asked, "What is happening to you?" For the first time, he revealed the fact that for the past few years he had been experiencing a flow of blood in his urine.

"This is a problem of immense emergency," I said, in tears. "You need to arrange an appointment with a physician as soon as possible."

His response was, "Can't you heal me?" I replied, "Yes! If you're willing to pray and study with me, you can expect healing!" "As an agnostic, I don't know that I am willing to do that," he said. "If not, then it is wiser for you to make an appointment with someone who can advise you as to the nature of the problem. Your needs must be addressed right away, Ron. You must handle this immediately!"

Sensing fear was responsible for Ron's neglect of his physical condition, I said, "Sickness is a temptation to believe that God's goodness and power aren't able to keep us safe and well. This belief causes fear. Healing is a result of one's own spiritual growth, a change of thought. It's a natural process, which comes as the result of increased understanding.

"Healing isn't a miracle. It isn't a case of one individual having a special source of power over another." And I repeated, "If you are willing to work with a Christian Science practitioner, study and pray, you can expect healing. The reason you believe you are an agnostic, Ron, is that you've never really addressed the inner questions: Why are we here? What is life all about?"

I instinctively knew Ron didn't have a lot of time. He had put up with this problem longer than he was willing to admit. I was sure his condition was one of the reasons we reconnected. I also knew he was too loving and intelligent a man to really doubt that God exists.

Ron was naturally confused about how prayer can change the physical condition. People often make the mistake of thinking spiritual healing is a miracle or something magic. It isn't dependent on person, place, or thing. Nothing has power but God. Healing results from gaining higher views of one's true selfhood, one's inseparability from the presence of God.

Christian Science teaches that there is in reality no life or intelligence in matter, and that illness is the result of entertaining (listening to) false, finite belief. It is our own material thinking, resistance to spiritual growth, and ignorance that seems to bring disease into our experience. When error is corrected in thought, the body responds to the wellness that is already true.

This rule is perfectly stated in the first chapter of Genesis: "God made man in His image and likeness." Most of us are educated to accept the second chapter of Genesis, a Biblical allegory, as reality. The allegory is the story of Adam and Eve, an imaginary account of the moment when our forefathers accepted the belief in a power opposed to God—the moment they lost their sense of connection with God's presence. It is nothing more than a myth, just as Christ Jesus proved.

Family began arriving for the day's celebration, so for the moment, we postponed the discussion. Nancy arrived with a friend. Shelley arrived with her husband, Curt Chaffee, and with them my stepdaughter, Jan Cost. It was an exquisite Sunday afternoon. For the first time, Ron met most of my precious family.

The sun was warm and beautiful. The flowers, plants, and trees around the patio were alive as though they were dancing with joy as we all sat around, visiting and enjoying Mother's Day together. I was thrilled and excited to have everyone together.

Ron's physical condition, however, was a huge concern. Whenever fear for Ron's condition came to my thought, I quietly affirmed spiritual truths about him. I reasoned over and over to myself that God does not bring His spiritual ideas together to cause them to lose one another. God is a loving God! The belief that God takes our loved ones away through illness and death is a false sense of God. It has its source in fear and lack of spiritual understanding.

Continuing to reason to myself, I affirmed man has a pre-existence, and eternal life is his present reality. We existed before we arrived here, and we will continue to experience life after we leave. Life is continuous. God is our Life. God didn't give us a life separate from Him. He gave us His Life, since as Paul says, "In him we live and move and have our being."

In further affirmation, I declared, in reality man has never been born into matter. The material world is an illusionary, counterfeit state of consciousness and existence. The basic error is not so much the belief of death out of a material existence as it is the belief of birth—the belief that we are born into matter.

Finding Ron was a gift, and I reaffirmed with all my heart that we would never be separated again, and since God is Love, He/She associates us with right ideas. God doesn't give us a precious relationship—a spouse or child— for the purpose of taking them away.

A verse came to me from Ecclesiastes 3: "*I know that, whatsoever God doeth, it shall be for ever: nothing can be put to it* [no evil can be added to it], *nor any thing taken from it* [nor any good removed from it]: . . ." I repeated this until it became a part of my deepest understanding.

Over the next couple of days, we toured the Monterey Peninsula. I showed him one of my favorite artist's fine art hanging in the lobby of the Pebble Beach Lodge. Exquisite paintings of Big Sur by Pebble Beach artist Van Megert, seven feet high by four feet wide, graced the walls. Ron loved each of them. Big Sur is a magnificent subject matter, and Megert is well known for that imagery. I also took him to a local gallery where I had introduced Megert's work to the owners. As a result, Megert had been exhibiting there for several years.

I met Van Megert, or Jerry, as his friends call him, in '82 when I was putting together fundraisers for JP's campaign for California State Assembly. Several artist friends contributed to the events.

Maggie Eastwood held a fundraiser in her Pebble Beach home. We were able to raise thousands of dollars from the sale of original artwork contributed by local Carmel artists, who were extremely kind and generous to JP's campaign.

While in Pebble Beach, Ron and I decided to have lunch at Roy's Restaurant at Spanish Bay. We had a delicious meal with plenty of quiet time for conversation. Afterward we sat out by the eighteenth green and enjoyed the beautiful white sands of the beaches, the view of Point Joe, and the golf course. We listened to the bagpiper who plays during the early evening hours.

As we sat quietly embracing one another in our thoughts, I glimpsed in Ron the real man of God's creating, totally free and independent of any belief in life, truth, or intelligence in matter. I glimpsed his genuine spiritual nature and being.

As we drove south along the 17 Mile Drive, I pointed to the home we previously owned on the thirteenth tee of the Monterey Peninsula Country Club Shore Course. Further south on the 17 Mile Drive, I showed him a lot we once owned across the street from the ocean with the back of it on the fourth hole of Spyglass Golf Course. It had a perfect view of Cypress Point to the south and Point Joe to the north.

Before I put him back on the plane to return home, we visited Cannery Row, the Monterey Aquarium, Pacific Grove, and the quaint art community Carmel-by-the-Sea.

We arrived at the Monterey Airport in plenty of time for Ron to catch his flight back to the John Wayne Airport in Orange County. We were both depressed. It was almost impossible to say goodbye. We had no idea when we would be able to see one another again. When it was time for him to walk to his flight, I went up on the upper deck to watch him board.

Since the plane sat on the ground for another twenty minutes, I had time to move my car to the upper parking area, where I watched the plane until it left the ground. Though my heart was sad to see him leave, my thought remained in total prayer for his safety, his health, and the next blessed event when we could reconnect again.

Summer 2003

Right Relationships

What greater way to celebrate the extended days and sunsets of summer than to spend them with the one you love? Thoughts like these were occurring to me as I speedily drove to Newport Beach from the Monterey Peninsula once again.

It was my third trip to see Ron, and I felt concerned. Because I didn't have all the information as to the full nature of his illness, it was still difficult to understand why he was unable to sit for any length of time and drive to Monterey.

One of our objectives during this visit was to contact the Julian Whitaker Institute of Wellness in Newport Beach and set up an appointment for a thorough exam. Since Ron hadn't seen a doctor in many years, he was extremely apprehensive. The physician with whom Ron made an appointment at Whitaker was Dr. Farrier, and he gave Ron good advice. He suggested a full body scan to determine the nature of his problem.

We made an appointment for the scan and learned within two hours that Ron had a cancerous tumor of the bladder and needed surgery as quickly as possible. Fortunately the tumor was encapsulated within the bladder. However, there was a question as to whether the cells were beginning to spread. The tumor was so large that it blocked one of his kidneys, causing it to atrophy, and partially blocked the other kidney. This was thought to be the source of his back and leg misery. With this knowledge, it was obvious why it was impossible for Ron to consider driving any distance at all.

We needed to get help as quickly as possible. Time was of the essence, because it was further learned, through the wisdom of Dr. Farrier, that Ron had had this condition for more than fifteen years.

It's hard to believe someone would avoid a problem as serious as his for any length of time. However, the more I became reacquainted with the boy I knew as a young girl, the more I understood why he had neglected taking care of himself.

Most of his reason for neglect of his own condition was fear—fear of hospitals and doctors. He also had a very ill wife to care for over a long period of time and found it convenient to postpone attention to his own physical needs. Ron was deeply devastated by the loss of his spouse after fifty-one years of marriage, and he was also deeply hurt by the loss of a great deal of his fortune due to an investment in a business outside of his profession and unrelated to his life's work.

After his wife, Jodi, passed on, Ron gave up the desire to fight for his life. My reconnecting with Ron again gave him a renewed sense of motivation—a desire to move beyond the illness rather than being consumed by it.

We both had been through insurmountable odds in our lives. Spiritual growth led my thought away from self, redirected my goals, and taught me how to have a generosity of spirit, in other words, how to accommodate, tolerate, and forgive myself and others. Spiritual growth gave me wonderful reasons to connect and love again.

Ron's reasons to love and be loved were different, but not too dissimilar. His father had multiple love affairs. Ron knew about them because, from the time he was a small child, his father often took him with him when he visited his girlfriends.

Ron's father frequently placed Ron in the precarious position of having to lie to his mother about his dad's activities. In order to protect her from the devastation of the truth, Ron was often forced to lie to his mother. This made Ron miserably unhappy. He loved both of his parents deeply, but it wasn't his nature to deceive anyone.

This was the primary reason behind his extreme unhappiness when he met his first wife, Jodeane. They met on a cruise to Hawaii. Ron was twenty-four and on the ship with his parents. Jodi was the same age and was traveling with her aunt and cousin. While together constantly for two weeks, they fell in love.

Jodi knew Ron had lost a lot of zest for life and promised to make him happy. What he never mentioned to her, what she never knew, was that he was upset and disgusted over his parents' marital relationship.

Ron hated the constant deception and bickering. He never explained the real reasons behind his depression to his future wife. He never even told her during the fifty-one years of their marriage.

Ron also didn't discuss his feelings and broken spirit regarding the business reversal—a business unrelated to his life's work—in a restaurant in Tucson with his wife, Jodi. He now wished he had. He wanted someone to be the spiritual and moral support he badly needed. He needed to share his disappointment. Neither Ron nor Jodeane Harrod had learned to share their deepest feelings.

To feel mentally distressed or agitated over physical or financial setbacks can be likened to a perpetual state of grief or anxiety. If we are not consciously forgiving ourselves for a mistake or decision, we remain constantly in the past and seldom enjoy the splendors of the moment.

The Dalai Lama writes in his *Little Book of Inner Peace* the following: "If a misfortune has already occurred, it is best not to worry about it, so we do not add fuel to the problem. Don't ally yourself with past events by lingering on them and exaggerating them. Let the past take care of itself, and transport yourself to the present while taking whatever measures are necessary to ensure that such a misfortune never occurs again, now or in the future."

Ron's unhappiness with his parents' marriage helped explain why we became more intimately involved than we should have as teenagers. Both of us were in extreme emotional pain, and loving one another gave us hope, soothed the depth of our wounds, and made it possible to face life on a daily basis.

Ours wasn't just a casual affair. In one another, we sought reason and sanity. Neither of us knew the full depth of our feelings at the time, but they were profound enough to be recalled by each of us over the many years we were separated. Now, fifty-six years later, we clearly understood our feelings for one another.

When Ron went away and we parted in our late teens, it broke my heart. The love I felt for him, however, gave me a quality of hope I never had before. The experience of knowing what it really meant to love another person gave me the desire and the courage to survive. Prior to that, I wasn't aware of feelings for anyone.

All I had known before loving Ron was immense fear and distrust. Our relationship showed me how to trust. It taught me how loving another human being can be a powerful motivation for life. Until then it was impossible to trust anyone. I couldn't. Trusting adults always had brought immense pain.

Finding the right physician came about due to the kindness of Dr. Farrier. He told Ron that several colleagues had mentioned that if they ever needed a urologist, they would go to Dr. Cu Phan in Newport Beach. We made an appointment as quickly as possible.

It was July before we could schedule an appointment. Ron's condition was getting worse. It was to the point where he needed me and wanted me to be with him.

Back in Carmel and over the phone, we discussed the possibility of my moving to Newport. My response was something like: "I love you very much, always have and always will. I won't just come and live with you, however."

He said he loved me and needed me. Ron asked if I would move to Newport Beach to become his wife. The answer to that question was obvious because he had never really been out of my thought or my heart all those years.

After giving the owners of Classic Art Galleries two weeks' notice, I made plans to move. It was sad to leave. I enjoyed working with the other art consultants and the owners more than any other gallery I had previously been associated with. The owners, Jovan Micovic and his wife, Sanya, were kind, thoughtfully loving, and supportive.

Fortunately, I didn't have much to move. Because I'd become a minimalist—scaling down my possessions for several years—the move progressed easily.

We were married in July by a judge, the Honorable Dewey Falcone, at Veterans Park in Redondo Beach, just a few days after I moved to Southern California. Shelley and her husband, Curt Chaffee, as well as Nancy attended our wedding. Ron's daughter Janeanne was there with her husband, Johnny Rinaldi. Ron's nephew by marriage, Mark Collins, flew in from Arizona. Pat Pollack Beall, a lifelong friend living in Manhattan Beach, also attended our small wedding.

During the first few months of our marriage we spent a lot of time in tears while sharing in further depth the details of our individual experiences during the many years we were separated.

I had a lot of prayer and spiritual study to do for myself. I was deeply grateful to be with Ron, but felt cheated due to the misunderstandings and lack of communication that led to the many years spent without him.

That attitude wasn't fair to his first family or mine! I knew better than to dwell on the past. I knew better than to allow resentment to become a part of our relationship. I refused to let insecurity have a foothold on the beginning of something beautiful.

Through prayer, I arrived at that peaceful place of gratitude for the life Ron had lived, the lovely person he chose to marry, and the beautiful family they enjoyed together. All sense of selfishness—the attitude of the small child from within—was eventually healed.

Ron married Jodeane (Jodi) Collins in 1952. Jodi's father was an attorney who became a member of the California State Assembly and eventually Speaker of the House. Her mother was Marjorie Maybel Deane Reynolds, the only daughter of Evert and Bessie Jane (Johnson) Reynolds. Bessie Jane's sister married Charles Chapman, founder of the Mission Orange Co. and Chapman College in the city of Orange.

Jodi Collins Harrod was the second cousin to the Fullerton Chapman family. Ron Harrod is a distant cousin to Johnny Appleseed Chapman.

Ron's father was Dr. "Bill" Clifford Camp Harrod. In the early '30s and for several years, Bill was mayor of Littleton, Colorado. Bill became an osteopath, eventually giving up his predilection for politics.

When Bill moved his family to California, he still needed an additional year of medical training to practice osteopathy there. Because it was the '30s and the country was still suffering from the Depression, he didn't have the means to finish medical school. So he began working as a chiropractor, and later, when he became more affluent, he opened several chiropractic offices in Southern California.

Ron's mother was Shirley Kathryn Ammerman. She married Bill Harrod in 1924. Shirley also became a chiropractor, and, for several years, she worked with Ron's father in his offices.

I have nothing but gratitude for the life Ron, Jodi, and their daughters enjoyed together. And I have the same sense of gratitude in my heart for the family life I've experienced.

Ron and I have always been in our right place. We were with the people we needed to be with. We both deeply loved our families. Our experiences taught us what we needed to learn and prepared us for a future life with one another.

I've had so many memorable events to be grateful for. Two marriages resulted in the birth of my precious daughters, Shelley and Nancy. They are two of the three most cherished people in my life, Ron being the third. Their presence never ceases to cause me to feel immense gratitude and joy for our relationship and the privilege of being their mom.

My relationships have forced me to thoroughly examine my thinking. Prayer and spiritual study have transformed my life and revealed more of who I am. And I have to say, looking back I no longer waste valuable energy being depressed because of what I've been through. It was not my fault! Instead, I'm proud of the deeper, more thoughtful person my experience has forced me to become.

Ron's parents, Dr.'s Bill and Shirley Harrod in the early 1950s

A Healing of Fear

Learning to Trust

It was nearly three months before we decided to work with the physician recommended to us by the Whitaker Institute. For a second opinion, we flew to the state of Washington to discuss Ron's condition with a doctor at the Tahoma Clinic. He verified the immediate need for surgery. We contacted the urologist, Dr. Phan. Ten hours of surgery occurred in October 2003. Dr. Phan was relatively positive that once the cancerous bladder and surrounding tissue were removed, if there was no invasion of cancer cells in the lymph nodes, Ron would not need chemo.

Since Ron had a very intelligent, caring doctor who was considered among his colleagues to be the very best, it wasn't the surgery that presented the biggest problem. The most difficult thing that played on Ron's thought was fear—fear of being in a hospital. Secondly, his fear made it difficult for him to trust a surgeon to operate and an anesthetist to administer an anesthetic.

Ron's parents were both physicians. As a young man growing up in an osteopathic family, he heard countless stories regarding mistakes made in hospitals by surgeons and anesthetists in operating rooms. Ron's sister, at the age of three, passed on in a hospital just three months before Ron's mother delivered him. Both of his parents later passed on in hospitals.

According to an article in the *AARP Bulletin*, about ninety thousand Americans die each year from infections contracted in hospitals. A hospital can become the most dangerous place for one to be if one is sick, which makes hospitalization itself a risk. Overcoming fear then becomes an important step for anyone who enters a hospital.

I thought deeply about what was ahead for Ron. I understood it wasn't a coincidence that I was in a position to offer support. Suggestions of fear occurring and reoccurring to Ron needed to be eradicated from his thought. I was convinced that my prayers could help guide Ron out of a state of fear and help him learn how to trust again.

I talked to Ron about Christian Science and its spiritual approach to healing. He was familiar with it due to the fact that his grandmother, Anna Camp Harrod, was a student of Christian Science. Though Ron respected and admired it, he didn't feel ready to rely on Christian Science for himself. I embraced his decision and supported him in it, while I surrounded him with my love. I felt God's love embracing him, too.

I wasn't able to give him the full spiritual treatment that I experienced in the healings revealed earlier in my story. It wouldn't have been fair to Ron or to the doctors to try to work with him in Christian Science since it would have pulled Ron and his thought in a very different direction than the treatment he chose. But by loving Ron and the doctors—including everyone involved in his surgery—I was able to help him overcome fear and feel God's presence and love with him, right there in the hospital.

Prior to the surgery, a minister stopped by Ron's room and left a pamphlet titled *The Healing Power of the 23rd Psalm*. Ron read it over and over: "The Lord is my shepherd; I shall not want. He maketh me to lie down in green pastures: he leadeth me beside the still waters. He restoreth my soul: he leadeth me in the paths of righteousness for his name's sake. Yea, though I walk through the valley of the shadow of death, I will fear no evil: for thou art with me; thy rod and thy staff they comfort me. Thou preparest a table before me in the presence of mine enemies: thou anointest my head with oil; my cup runneth over. Surely goodness and mercy shall follow me all the days of my life: and I will dwell in the house of the Lord for ever."

Fear was the only enemy. By the time Ron was ready for surgery, he knew every word of the 23rd Psalm. Courage and peace gently replaced what could have been a paralyzing sense of fear.

The surgery lasted from two in the afternoon to midnight. The next morning, Dr. Curry, the anesthetist, came into Ron's room early. Ron was awake and grateful to be alive.

Dr. Curry told us that, in all the years he had practiced, Ron's operation was the most beautiful piece of surgery he had ever seen. He said it was a textbook case and should have been filmed for classroom instruction.

Before Ron left the hospital, however, something strange started to occur. One specialist after another stopped by his room to suggest he may have other complications. First it was a heart specialist. Then it was an oncologist. The gastroenterologist stopped by, and then another M.D. suggesting an MRI.

The list grew until we realized that this would continue as long as we allowed it.

It became obvious that it was time to take a stand for Ron's individual rights as a patient and to put an end to being tempted by fear and the various suggestions that he might have other complications.

Ron was there for a specific purpose. He had already been in surgery twice. The first time was an attempt to remove the tumor without major surgery. He had already had two events with the anesthetist. It could have been dangerous for him to have a third.

Each physician visiting him after surgery suggested there might be other complications. And each wanted to perform some new kind of test. In one case, the specialist wanted Ron to go back into surgery to perform an exploratory examination.

A full-body scan, as well as thorough examinations by two fully qualified physicians before Ron saw Dr. Phan, totally verified that except for the bladder cancer Ron was in perfect health. One of the doctors told us, for instance, that he had the heart of a forty-year-old man.

The various doctors who came to Ron's hospital room seemed to us to be persons attempting to "sell their wares." Their reasons for suggesting Ron might have further complications were just supposition. There was no proof of further need for doctoring or medication.

Ron and I discussed this at length and made the decision to assert his rights as a patient. We called the cancer physician, Dr. Phan, and asked him to inform the desk that Ron was ready to be released from the hospital.

After two and a half weeks, Ron left the hospital and returned home free of cancer, free of fear, and filled with trust. He had a whole new beginning and a new sense of faith in God and his fellow man. We finally had ahead of us a life of love to celebrate with one another.

Reconnecting with Ron took place in 2003. It's now five years later, and my heart continues to be grateful that Ron felt led to search for me and found me.

I feel such happiness to finally have the life I've wanted to live, the quality of relationship I've dreamed of, and a husband who cherishes his marriage.

And I am grateful to have reached the level of confidence I've needed to feel within myself. It's been my life's work to connect with my peaceful center. What better work could I have chosen? For what greater result could I have hoped?

Conclusion

In my own thought, as I was willing to stop listening to and entertaining voices of fear and lack of self-worth, in that proportion, I found myself experiencing greater dominion, a peaceful and more satisfying life.

Preoccupation with the past can make one oblivious to the present good. Gandhi advised: "Always aim at purifying your thoughts and everything will be well." And he further advised: "The weak can never forgive. Forgiveness is the attribute of the strong."

Forgiving myself for a lack confidence in my own self-worth enabled me to take the next step and forgive others.

Forgiveness is an essential step in the process of healing. It's something we do, not so much for the other individual as for ourselves—to free ourselves.

Withholding forgiveness keeps disappointment and anger alive. And those deflections of thought can keep us in a chronic state of depression, while forgiveness purifies our thought, mind, and body. It *restores* us from the core of our being—our soul outward.

Whether it is verbal or physical, childhood abuse changes who we are and what we may become. Recognizing and addressing our issues enables us to heal. Without healing, we may never know our own uniqueness.

Eckhart Tolle wrote in his most recent book, *A New Earth*: "There is only one perpetrator of evil on the planet: human unconsciousness. That realization is true forgiveness. With forgiveness, your victim identity dissolves, and your true power emerges—the power of Presence. Instead of blaming the darkness, you bring in the light."

At times, I've had to deliberately face my thought and ask myself the question: do you want to feel the peace that is possible, or do you want to keep reacting to the selfish thought that deprives yourself and others around you of the blessings at hand?

Though I wasn't the source of the terror, I was a vessel of hate and sadness as the result of my experience. And those thoughts kept me in a state of depression and made my whole body ill.

"When, at some point in our lives, we meet a real tragedy, we can react in one of two ways," wrote the Dali Lama. "Obviously, we can lose hope and let ourselves slip into despair, into alcohol, drugs, and unending sadness. Or else we can wake ourselves up, discover in ourselves an energy that was hidden there, and act with greater clarity and more force."

Sadness for a lost childhood, a youth stripped of dignity and burdened by shame, has been forever silenced—*redeemed by Love*—through prayer and spiritual growth in my life.

I owe everything I've become, every affirmation of spiritual reality declared, what I've learned about healing, and the gratitude I feel primarily to two books: The Holy Bible and *Science and Health with Key to the Scriptures* by Mary Baker Eddy. Study and spiritual growth brought with it the promised comfort.

The love, support, patience, and understanding received from my immediate family, as well as Christian Science practitioners and close friends, have also richly contributed to the many healings I've experienced.

Gandhi has summed up my feelings: "Be the change you want to see in the world."

Left to right standing are RUHS friends: Rosalie Fritzen, Carol Cameron, Sharri Rodecker, Basil Cunningham, BettyJo Root, Sally Anne Masury, and Beverly Husted; seated are Maureen O'Connor, Jacque Elerding, Susie Jones, and Patti Gibson in a 1948 *Daily Breeze* photograph.

Contact us

BettyJo Cost	bettyjocost@me.com
Website	www.bettyjocost.com
Website	www.JamesPeterCost.com
S.L. "Ron" Harrod	rhadvice@aol.com
Shelley A. Cost	www.shelleycost.com
Curtis Wilson Cost	www.costgallery.com

Let the redeemed of the Lord say so, whom he hath redeemed from the hand of the enemy.

Psalms 107:2